Stop Slicing,
Start Playing…
Your Best

Joseph K. Sullivan

www.noslice.com

ISBN# 1-58320-005-3

Cover design by Ronnie Mesa
Interior layout by Lifestyles Press
Special thanks to: Henri Forget, Bruce Marcho
Photographs of Tom Watson, Nick Price, Ernie Els,
and Colin Montgomerie: Dave Cannon
Photographs of Greg Norman and
Lee Trevino: Dom Furore

Trademarks: noslice.com®, The SELFish Four®

Foreword

I have never been a great golfer. I will probably never be a great golfer, either. Yet I have seen both sides of the average player's coin. I have experienced misery, and I have tasted success.

Most importantly, through the myriad ups and downs, and the constant struggle with a fragile psyche, I have achieved a peace with this game. Yes indeed, after fifteen years of playing, I have come to realize why I truly love the game of golf.

For me, golf is about...
...getting out of the house,
...getting the fellas together,
...playing for a buck a hole,
...sweeping the dew off the grass,
...reminiscing high school,
...eating dogs at the turn,
...relaxing in the sun,
...talking Red Wings hockey,
...good for good,
...winning the bet. That's cool!

That's just me. That may or may not be you. Your outlook on the game may be completely different. Maybe it's your goal to be the club champion someday. Maybe it's to break 100 for the first time. Maybe you just want to be able to enjoy a game with your husband or wife on a Sunday afternoon.

No matter what your goals are in regard to this great game of golf, they start here. I must say that the reason I enjoy golf today is because of what is taught in this book. I am confident that you can find your own peace with this game, and enjoy it to the fullest, by applying what is expressed over the following collection of pages.

Your time has come.
Enjoy.

Joseph K. Sullivan

Contents

Introduction

By now, you have probably scanned through the book a bit to get a sense of what it's about. You also, I'm sure, have some questions on your mind as you begin reading. You are probably wondering who this person in all of these photographs is.

Well, that's me, Joe Sullivan. I am the founder of *noslice.com*. I am the one who will try to help you become a better player.

You may be wondering what my credentials are.

Oh, boy, the list of great players I have taught is so long that it would fill an entire book to mention them all. Tiger, The Shark, and all the great players constantly try to seek me out to share my wisdom. The golf schools that want to hire me because of my expertise? *Holy smoke!* That list reads like a Charles Dickens novel. The magazine editors and book publishers? *Jeez o' peets!* I almost forgot to mention them. They are fighting over me.

Okay, I'm just kidding, obviously. My credentials are not a whole lot to speak of. As a matter of fact, now that I think of it, I am not even sure why I feel qualified to write this book. Let's see: I golf. I watch golf. I like to comment on golf. That's about it.

You may be wondering what this book is about.

Ultimately, this book is about eliminating your slice and improving your golf game. *Ultimately,* I say, because it takes a little while to get there, as I see it necessary to give some background information on myself for the first few pages.

I feel it to be of the utmost importance for people to know some of the history behind myself and my golf game. It's not because I am dying to write an autobiography or something. I just think it has to do with that whole trust thing. It wouldn't be fair if I just came out of the gates with some magic formula that may or may not help you improve your game. There must be a purpose behind what I say, and a reasoning to go along with it. That is what you will learn in Part I.

If, however, you aren't interested in how my methods were developed, feel free to skip ahead to Part II, which covers the core of the book, the instruction. This section illustrates what you do wrong in your swing, and how you can correct it. You will find that how you correct it is with *The SELFish Four*.

The final section is what I would call half-instruction, half-commentary. It's kind of my sarcastic, broad-based look at certain areas of the game and how they may be affecting you. I hope it will open your eyes to various aspects of the swing that you may not have been aware of.

Also keep in mind, as you will hear me say again, that I am not a harsh critic of golf instruction. Although some of the content near the end may suggest otherwise, I truly hope you believe this when you are finished reading. All I want to do is put my thoughts out there in the most entertaining and knowledgeable way I know possible, and hope you become a better player because of it.

PART 1

• • •

HOW IT
ALL BEGAN

▶ 1 ◀

"The journey begins."
—*E.J. Parker*

*I*t was May 1996. I had just been graduated from the University of Detroit and had to find a job fairly soon. I hadn't played golf in a while because of all the schoolwork demands near the end of the year. After school was over, I decided to hang out and play over the summer. I viewed it as sort of a reward for my hard work in school. In the fall, I would then decide how I was going to approach the rest of my life.

It seemed that all I needed was a short break from the game to rekindle my interest. No matter what the situation, golfers always seem to keep coming back for more. I'm certainly no different.

With my mind cleared and the worry over a swing-method relapse gone, I was ready to play again, and with my college degree in hand, I knew there were no worries or hurries because I would always have something to fall back on.

My game had suffered greatly, though I wanted to rebuild it. I had gone from a 2-handicap to a 19-handicap by the time I decided to put a stop to the direction my golf swing was headed. I knew the only way I was going to get better would be to find another way. I hoped that a new approach would not only lower my score, but also the level of embarrassment that I had been dealing with for what seemed like forever.

It was still hard for me to grasp what I was doing for the previous two years of my life. The entire experience went deeper than just the loss of a swing. When I finally called it quits, I sat down and evaluated the situation. It was apparent that during that time span from May 1994 through May 1996, everything was a negative. I had lost confidence. I had lost a golf game. I had lost money. I had lost respect. I had lost self-esteem. I even lost friends whom I used to play with.

Even with all of those losses, the most important thing I lost was time—not just the time I spent for two years trying to overhaul my swing, but the time I could have been doing something productive. Instead of taking small steps forward, I took a major step back. Regardless, it was old news by then, and there was no use sulking anymore.

The Change

In May 1994, I decided to completely change my golf swing. My game was not getting any better, and I never had much of a textbook swing to begin with. I felt that by developing a more technically-sound move, I would improve my ball striking, or, at the very least, I would have a swing that appeared more conventional.

Up to that point, I never had much of an understanding about the mechanics of the swing. Growing up, I didn't concern myself with anything technical. I was a total "feel" player who basically developed a natural, homemade swing. There was the occasional *Golf Digest* piece, but that's about it. I figured, however, that if I were to get my game to the level I wanted it at, I needed to make some significant changes.

I chose to focus my attention on some popular swing beliefs that were surfacing at the time. They revolved around *keeping the arms connected to the body* and *swinging with the body.* Many touring pros were achieving great things by applying these methods, so I figured I would, too.

I worked religiously on these methods from the summer of '94 through the spring of '95: watching videos, hitting balls, reading books, occasionally taking lessons. As long as there wasn't snow on the ground, I was out on the range or the course. If it was 30 degrees, then so be it. If I could see the ball, I was there.

● ● ●

During these months of making changes, my mindset toward the swing had become very mechanical. Having never been that way, I didn't realize the adverse effects that thinking this way can have on a "feel" player such as myself. It was all new to me: the terminology, the thoughts, the positions. All these aspects of the swing that at one time meant very little, were now occupying my entire thought process, and beginning to harm my game.

It got to the point where I couldn't sit at home for more than two minutes, it seemed, before I had to fiddle with my swing. I would do drills for hours in my basement. I would even do drills in my ice-cold garage. I read that certain tour players had the feeling on their backswing that they were "starting a lawnmower." This would give them an athletic takeaway from the ball and put their right arm in good position at the top. So I would be out in the garage, with snow on the ground, yanking a lawnmower cord. *Sick!*

I would also make myself work with video on at least one aspect of my swing every night. Right in my family room I would set up my camcorder. I would use some balls I made out of masking tape and start ripping away. I must have thought I was hitting good shots because I couldn't see them land. No way, José! At least one positive came out of it all...I never broke anything.

I was becoming so insanely meticulous that I would actually talk into the camera about what swing thoughts I was going to use for that particular shot. I would say something such as, "Shift straight back, then feel like you're thumbing a ride on the downswing." (It's one of those things that would have been embarrassing if someone heard me.) I would then race downstairs to watch the tape I had just shot. A couple of minutes later, thinking I had it figured out, I would run back upstairs and do it all over again, with some new swing thoughts, of course. It was very silly and very stupid. My swing was really starting to crumble away.

Getting Worse

After the spring of '95, I was playing poorly, but even with my handicap rising faster than a South Florida dewpoint, I was still determined to get it right. I continued to work at my new swing throughout the summer. I hit countless range balls, trying to figure things out. I smacked bucket after bucket of balls, with each shot having an entirely different set of swing thoughts. Once again, I couldn't hit more than an occasional good shot. Every now and then, I would try some crazy thought and it would work. I would instantly get excited and think for a moment I had it figured out, but each time it was short-lived, as I came to realize that it's impossible to be consistent with all these thoughts racing through your head.

All this thinking led to even more problems. I became timid and lost all aggressiveness with my swing. I was hitting the ball nowhere and lucky if my swing speed reached the 90-mph range. This was obvious with every club in my bag. At one time I could rip a sand wedge about 110 yards, now I was lucky to hit it 75. Also, I became rather "bunt-like" with my driver; that is, my pure drives now topped out at about 230 yards.

At times, I really wanted to quit. I wanted to end this chapter of my life, finish up school, and move on from there. Besides, what was the point of all this? I was not going to become a pro golfer. Even if I were an exceptional player, the odds of becoming a pro, and making a living at it, are slim and none. I was going to be a two-to-three-times-per-month player once I was graduated and found a job. I could have used the time to read some good books or volunteer somewhere. Certainly some form of self-betterment could have been found away from golf.

Still, I was caught up in the entire buzz of it all. Seeing dozens of golfers improve their games with these methods had kept me coming back for more, and the belief I had in what I was practicing made me think that it was just a matter of time before I figured it out as well.

▶ 2 ◀

"I have nothing to offer but blood, toil, tears, and sweat."
—*Sir Winston Churchill*

Tournament Time

It was nearing the end of summer and I was itching to play in a tournament. My game was in no shape to be playing tournament golf, but there are some events that are just too much fun not to play in. The Michigan Match Play Championship is one of these events.

I entered just in time. I figured I would practice really hard right before it started, something would click, and I would be able to compete. I felt I was due for something good to happen.

Unfortunately, it didn't quite work out that way. I swear I must have tried a thousand swing thoughts during that event. Each thought seemed to result in an even uglier shot than the one before.

There is one shot I will never forget from that week. It was my drive the first day on the 17th hole at the host course, The Pines. I hit it so far right that it actually went out of bounds on this hole. Anyone who has ever played that course has probably never even noticed that there is O.B. right on 17. It was at least 100 yards right of the fairway. It was nasty, and symbolic of the entire tournament, for me.

My tournament ended quickly; I was eliminated in the first round. As I exited the course for the final time, I was worse than ever before. While walking out to my car after shaking the hand of my opponent, I didn't know if I should cry, or find the nearest bridge to jump off. In a way I felt sad, like a puppy left out in the rain, and in a way I was really pissed off! I actually looked up at the clear blue sky and murmured, "You have got to be kidding me" (with a few additional choice words); I traveled all the way up here for this torture?"

I thought about all the time and hard work I had committed to my new swing, and I was amazed that my game could have reached such a dismal state. I thought about what might have been had I done things a different way. I thought about what it used to be like to hit good shots. I thought about many things as I leaned up against the back of my car.

Perhaps the most spontaneous of things I thought about was all the money I had been squandering while trying to improve. The books, the videos, the lessons, the training gadgets, the range balls, the green fees; the list goes on. Whatever I felt would help my game I did not hesitate to buy.

In spite of this, as I think about it today, more than three years after the fact, I realize money is of relatively little consequence in the grand scheme of things, at least not when the most precious of all commodities, time, has also been lost. This, once again, is the hardest loss to deal with. I would accept much of what has become of this if I could simply have those two years back. I guess I could live with being a total hack and flat broke if I could have had an opportunity to utilize, in full, all the precious moments we have on earth (especially being twenty-one and in college).

●●●

I played in a couple more events during the summer and fall of 1995 with similar results. Not only was I a poor golfer by then, but I was quickly becoming a pariah of sorts with a few of my buddies from junior golf. Some of the really good players whom I competed with in high school didn't know what to say when I would post a 92. They were not sure if they should run and hide, or offer condolences. It truly was an awkward situation for all of us.

Nothing was working. I had become so confused with all the aspects of the swing. A method that I hoped would free my mind of mechanical swing thoughts, had done just the opposite. I was paralyzed through the constant analysis of every move. Was I shifting my weight enough? Staying connected? Squeezing a nut? Thumbing a ride? Standing like a weightlifter? Keeping the club in front of my body? Rotating my trunk? Staying level?

The Problem

After the tournament season ended, I knew I had to try something different. I was desperate, and would have done anything to start hitting the ball better. I just knew I could no longer keep doing the same things I had been and expect to improve.

I went out to the range and started experimenting, which was something I had done almost daily. Only this time, to my dismay, my horrifying slice, which is the basis of this book, really came to fruition. Up until then, I was hitting a combination of chunks, quick hooks, skulls, and slices, but once I began moving my upper body laterally on the downswing even more than I already was, a weak slice became commonplace.

As I think back while writing this, I get this rather enigmatic feeling about how much I began moving laterally through the shot. Out of all the crazy swing ideas I tried, could this have been what pushed things over the edge? Could this have been what said sayonara to any chance I had of playing good golf? Could this have been what led to my first three-digit score that I can remember?

Certainly, there is no question that my game had reached such a sad state from my entire experience over those two years, but if there were one instance I could pinpoint as being more detrimental than any other, it would have to be this large lateral move of my upper body that I developed during the downswing.

I remember doing "the Gary Player drill," where he walks through the ball after he hits it. I would lunge so far forward just so I would make sure I walked through the ball. It was the most unnatural feeling ever, but after reading about the benefits it can bring, I was convinced it would help my game.

While doing this drill, I would approach the ball from such a steep angle. The first couple of shots I stuck the club right into the ground and barely made contact. Once I did make clean contact, I would produce so much left-to-right spin on the ball that it would result in a weak slice. This was because in an effort to walk through it, my head and shoulders were moving laterally and opening up a great deal, and there is a significant loss of power and direction when these things happen. I wish, before then, that I had seen photos of every great player at impact. They all have their head behind the ball, and they all form a concave bow with the right side of their body, at impact.

There were some other moves I was trying that really started to create the ultimate over-the-top sensation that signaled the end of whatever decent amateur golf career I might have had. After a year and a half into my quest to rebuild my golf swing, I knew that all hope was officially lost. It wasn't going to happen for me as long as I was doing what I was doing. I had to get out, or I would be forever held in a tangled web of swing ideas.

The Final Straw

I was pretty dejected for the first couple of months of 1996. Golf was, for a change, the furthest thing from my mind. It was the middle of another cold winter in Michigan and there were plenty of things I could occupy my time with other than the constant focus on the golf swing.

I had only one semester left in college and I sure didn't want to blow everything I had achieved to that point. I figured I would concentrate on school and take a long sabbatical from the game to let my physical and mental trauma heal. I could then reevaluate things and see if golf was still right for me. The problem was, I screwed up again.

I decided to go to Pinehurst with the University of Detroit golf team, of which I was a part-time member. It was during our spring break, and I guess I had nothing better to do. Instead of going up north skiing and having some fun, I decided to punish myself further by playing more golf. It's not that I didn't want to go play several rounds of golf in one of the premier golf destinations in the world, it was that I could barely make contact with the ball.

We went down the first week in March 1996 and played about ten rounds. What a golfer's paradise that area of North Carolina is. We teed off on some of the best courses in the country: The Pit, Pinehurst #7, Talamore; the list goes on. We were totally enamored with all this golf and some neat little cottages to stay in.

Although the golf courses and amenities were quite nice, the problem was that I think my lowest score was a 94. My performance was so sad that I don't even think I would consider what I was doing playing golf. It was more like *"mindless slapping of a white ball on grass."*

I had numerous swing thoughts racing through my mind every day. We played 36 holes a day, and each one was a disaster. You can multiply 36 by about 10 and that is the amount of swing thoughts I had per day. The rounds could not end fast enough. I just kept saying to myself, "Why am I out here?"

I was thoroughly embarrassed, not only for myself, but also for the U of D team. Here I was playing Pinehurst #7, one of the best courses in the world, and I had *no clue* where the ball was going. I was having such a miserable time on the course that I really had no desire to play. All I wanted to do was go back to my room and play some cards.

Fortunately, the trip was cut short because of weather. That was a relief. I never enjoyed the site of nonstop rain and 40-degree temperatures so much. It put me out of my golfing misery. On the way home, I knew something had to change, or I would have to quit playing for good.

▶ 3 ◀

"The times they are a-changin."
—Bob Dylan

*E*ven with all of my swing-related problems, I still wanted to improve my game. It seems that no matter how bad things can get with this game, there is still something indescribably great about hitting a pure golf shot. I just knew that if I were to ever hit another one, I'd have to find a different way.

I was done for good with the swing changes I had been working on for the previous two years. I realized that my body, my tempo, and my overall feel for the swing were not compatible with what I was trying to do. It may have worked for others, but not for me.

Through all the practice and lessons, I had accomplished nothing. I had started doing some of the worst moves imaginable in my swing. The excessive weight shift I had developed in my swing—of eight inches back, then fourteen inches through—had basically made me a beginning golfer all over again, and the sight of such lazy arms on my backswing had garnered a host of critics, as well as filling my life with chagrin. It was from these two moves that I had developed the biggest over-the-top slice there is.

I continually wondered if golf was over for me. *Is this it? Can I ever get back to a level of respectability with my game?* These were a couple of questions I asked myself after the experience ended. I was realistic because I knew my swing had become so mechanical. The instinctive player I had been throughout most of my golfing life was someone I was no longer familiar with. I knew the game would be forever difficult after being so consumed with every detail in the swing, but I never gave up.

Still Psycho

Just because I was done with a certain swing method, it did not necessarily mean that I was through with lessons altogether. I was still very entrenched in the mechanics of the swing. As much as I wanted to be a "feel" player once again, it's so hard to go back. *It's a disease.* Thinking mechanically, in my belief, is one of the worst brain diseases you can have. To have an infatuation with the way things work, and the nuances of how they are put together, at least in regard to the golf swing, is not healthful. As much as I tried to convince myself to do away with these thoughts, my "disease" became worse.

I often compared my "mechanicalness" in golf with the way I approached other sports. I wondered why I couldn't play golf with the mindset with which I had in those sports. When I used to play lacrosse and would go to throw a ball, I sure didn't think:

"Hold the stick with your hands fifteen inches apart; set your feet closed to the target; rotate the head of the stick back with its angle matching your left arm pad; slide your weight forward while sticking your elbow into the number on your jersey; from there just release and finish in a well-balanced position with the head of the stick pointing in the direction just below and to the right of the intended target."

Of course I didn't think this way. I just looked at the target that I was going to pass it to or shoot it at, and let it go.

This is how I used to play golf when I was younger. It used to be just grip it and rip it. It used to be just tee it high and let it fly. Not anymore, though. Not in the present day. Not with my mind being in the paralyzing state of fear that it was. Not with my swing being the result of a complete saturation of analysis.

I tried to go back to the swing I was using before, certainly, but to no avail. When I used to swing that way naturally, without thinking about it, that was fine. My tempo, speed, and mechanics all flowed together and I was able to produce some good, consistent shots. Now I tried to swing like my old self while being conscious of the mechanics I once had, which was not a good idea. It was disastrous, so I knew that was not a possibility.

Because I was this way, I felt I needed more professional help to improve. I investigated some of the local Michigan pros to find someone who was good. The problem was that I didn't know who was considered good. I never really followed the golf-lesson scene to get a feeling of who the hot instructor was. As a result, I had to rely on the recommendations of other students.

With the advice of a couple of buddies of mine, I decided to take some lessons from John Koch and Ron Beurmann. These guys are fine instructors who helped me a great deal. They took care of some major problems with my technique that reduced my slice significantly. John had me keep my head behind the ball at impact. Before, my head was going forward about 6-8 inches on the downswing before I struck the ball, and leading to all sorts of problems. John told me to feel as though I moved my head to the *right* at the start of my downswing. This is what many pros, knowingly or not, do in their swings as well.

Ron had me keep my right shoulder back, instead of throwing it over the top. I remember our lesson together as if it were yesterday. He would stand in front of me and put his club on my right shoulder. This would prevent me from moving my right shoulder over the plane, and would put me in a good position at impact. I hit it really well that day.

So there definitely were some good things that came out of these lessons. I was once again hitting the ball on the grooves and seeing a glimmer of hope for my future ball striking ability. As you might expect, however, all was not great. I would hit a few good shots, then follow those with a nasty slice. I was still far too technical. I was thinking of all the aspects of the swing at once and was very tentative because of it. I needed to have a swing where I could be more natural and aggressive, something that would allow me to just stand up to the ball, be confident, and rip the hell out of it!

Thanks, Mom

Life is filled with a lot of weird and ironic events. For me, one of these happened with a book my mom bought me for my 17th birthday. The book was titled, *Cure Your Slice Forever*, by John Huggan. I never even opened it up when I first got it. It was one of those presents that you sort of laugh at when you receive it. *"A book for slicers. Are you kidding me?"* I would say to myself. This was a book for total hacks, I thought. I did not need it because I was playing great at the time and definitely did not have a slice, but my mom doesn't know golf from football, so she figured anything golf related would make me happy, which it usually did.

It's funny that this book taught me more about the golf swing than I thought I could ever know. Five years after my 17th birthday, and because I was still suffering the effects of a huge, over-the-top slice, I decided to open up this still new, but dusty, book. I really had to swallow my pride to open up some book written for slicers.

As I thumbed through this masterpiece, I started to get a clear picture of what actually needs to happen in the swing to get the ball from point A to point B. The plane, clubface positions, and various other things all started to make sense. The illustrations and explanations as to what causes a slice were eerily similar to the problems I had in my swing.

Up to that point, I never had much of an understanding about these essential moves in the swing. When I was in the midst of revamping my game, all I cared about were the areas of the swing relevant to the method I was working on. Everything else was blocked out of my mind. The few lessons after were good, only they were more of the quick-fix variety. Not anymore, though. Not with this book. Things were starting to come into focus. The game was all of a sudden becoming cool again.

Bye Bye Slice

The next time I went out to the range I tried some of the drills in the book. Instantly, things started to get better. Once I grasped the concept of swing path and plane, I knew what I had to do to eliminate my slice. I knew I could no longer throw the club over the plane if I wanted to hit good shots. Instead, I had to come from the inside, like 99.9% of all the Tour pros do. The drill that was mentioned about swinging outside a shaft on the backswing, then inside it on the downswing, made this inside move so easy and understandable.

It still bothers me to this day that, when I was reconstructing my swing, I could never grasp a better understanding of this dropping of the club to the inside. This is the most important part of the swing. This is why some people are playing on TV and others are playing tennis. This is what I found out the hard way.

I continued to work on these drills and started hitting some good shots once again. I would use variations of some of the things that were talked about in Mr. Huggan's book. I found that I could place this broken shaft (or dowel stick) in the ground farther away from my right foot, and play a nice fade. I would still swing outside the stick on the backswing, then inside it on the downswing, but I would cut across the ball enough to fade it. Or I would put the stick closer to my right foot to play a big draw. This would force me to approach the ball way from the inside and, in turn, create an abundance of right-to-left spin, which led to the draw. Whatever I did with this drill, it seemed to work.

Perhaps the neatest thing about swinging around this stick in the ground was that it eliminated many of the mechanical thoughts that were racing through my mind. I knew that if I swung outside the stick on the way back, and inside it on the way down, then everything else would take care of itself. I no longer had to think about leg action, hip action, wrist action, torso action, etc. All these elements of the swing seemed to happen naturally.

Moreover, I could use the stick thoughts on the golf course. I would stand up to the ball and visualize the stick being there. Then I would simply imagine swinging outside it, then inside it. There were no more four or five thoughts per shot. It was one thing, which would automatically put me in good positions, and allow me to be aggressive.

• • •

In addition to the drills in this book, I essentially went about learning the proper moves in the golf swing in reverse, in a way. What I mean by that is this...When you do what it takes to hit awful golf shots, which I was doing, it can sometimes give you a much better understanding of what needs to be done in order to hit good shots. *"Say what?"* It really can if you allow your mind to be objective and critical of the things you are doing wrong.

For a long while I was not that way, and that is why I never improved. I was set on a method, and nothing was going to deter me from that, but as soon as I allowed myself to say, "Gee, Joe, those are some rather awful positions to be in," I started to get some good results.

When I looked at video of my swing, I saw someone who had an extreme amount of lateral motion with his body, and a completely disastrous over-the-top path and plane structure to his golf swing. That said, I could assume that a quieter body and a steep, then shallow swing path and plane structure would probably help. I would also look at my takeaway position. I had kind of a three-piece backswing with very little extension, and a bent left arm at the top of my swing. To prevent this, I would focus on swinging the club back lower to the ground. This would give me nice extension, width, and arc, and result in a much better position at the top of my swing. These were the types of things I started doing.

A Common Theme

Cure Your Slice Forever, as well as my reflections on the past, certainly had me thinking the right things about the golf swing again. I must say they definitely enhanced my cerebral approach to the swing. However, it was not until I intently analyzed the swing that I really grasped what was necessary in order to play good golf. X's and O's are fine in terms of reference points, but it all comes down to how things are executed by the ones who do it the best.

I started to take a close look at some of the great players' swings. I studied and studied and it seemed that there was one thing that all non-slicing players had in common. It was that they all swung relatively steep (outside) on the backswing and shallow (from the inside) on the downswing. No matter what grip, stance, tempo, posture, or length of swing they had, they all swung the club back steep, then down shallow, which is the exact opposite of swinging over the top. This put them all in the correct inside position where they could attack the ball. From this position, they could play a draw, a fade, or hit it straight.

I came to the conclusion that the only way I was going to hit good shots on a consistent basis was to swing down from the inside the way practically every professional I looked at did. Just as importantly, I knew I would never be able to play well if I went back to swinging over the top. As you will see, this is the reason for the emphasis on swing path and plane in my teaching system.

Conclusion

I took the knowledge I had gained from a couple of months of studying, reading, analyzing, and opening my mind to common sense. From there, I knew I had it figured out. I knew what there was to know about the swing. I realized that some things you don't have to know because everyone does them differently, but some things you do need to know because they are essentials. I knew that if *I* could start to play well again after the over-the-top slice I had developed, then certainly others could also. It was time for me to look firmly at what I was doing, and develop it into a system that would help any slicer. *Noslice.com* and *The SELFish Four* were soon formed, and it was time to let the world know about them.

Part II

• • •

NOSLICE.COM PHILOSOPHY

► 4 ◄

"We are not retreating – we are advancing in another direction."
—*General Douglas MacArthur*

*N*ow that you know some of the history behind my golf game and *noslice.com*, it's time to learn my system. In this section, my entire teaching philosophy will be laid out in detail. I will show you why you slice, and how you can correct it, in some very simple ways. *No confusing jargon. Just simple stuff.*

Before I proceed, though, there is one more thing that may be of interest to you, one more piece to the puzzle that has created this teaching thingamajig. That is the name. Why the name? Why *noslice.com?* Why a "dot com" name in an industry where the game is played on grass?

Good question. I'm not too sure. I just thought it was pretty neat. I was in search of something that was not too boring, but which would also underscore the intentions of the philosophy. I didn't want to just name it *Joey's Golf Stuff* or *End Your Slice.* It had to be somewhat hip, somewhat tech-savvy, and also let people know that this was a place where *slicers* could come for help.

Make no mistake; my main intention is to help the slicer (and/or high handicapper), although what my system entails can help every single player. Although what I talk about, especially this "steep, then shallow, swinging down from the inside" move, are the fundamentals that are essential to every non-slicing swing, I want to help slicers, especially the anguished over-the-top slicers. These are the majority of golfers in the world, and these are the ones who need my help the most.

This is not a place where a 1-handicapper should come and expect to become a Tour pro. A 1-handicapper most likely has the essential foundations already in place in his or her swing. There is not a lot more that needs to be known by this player. If they want to make the next step, it's now just a matter of how much talent they have, practicing their butt off, and getting lucky.

Instead, this is a place for the high-handicapper, who doesn't have anything close to the essential foundations in the swing. It is for those who have so ingrained that horrifying slice move into their swing, and as much as they have tried, can't seem to get rid of it. I want to get those players' handicaps in the single digits, *fast!*

● ● ●

My instructional methods focus on the necessary elements of the golf swing. I have looked at the greatest non-slicing players in the world to see what they have in common in their swings to produce straight, non-slicing shots. From Byron Nelson to Tom Watson to Matt Kuchar, you will find these swing characteristics present. I try to not focus on the individual aspects of their swings, such as tempo and length of swing, that make them and you unique. I just want you to take from their swings what makes them good, not what makes them an individual.

If you would like to hear about various intangibles in the swing, such as linkage, lever angles, connection, supination, pivot positions, centrifugal force, radii, or X-factors, then this is not the book for you. Perhaps *The Physics of Golf* or *The Science of the Golf Swing* is more what you are looking for. Here I talk about only what's most important, while, I hope, doing so in an easily understandable manner.

In an effort to make things as simple as possible, I focus my teaching philosophy around swing path and plane, and a little clubface positioning. These are the key components in the swing and the moves that all players need to hone before anything else needs attention. I will illustrate later in this book why these are the only things that matter.

What the whole swing basically comes down to is…if you do not have the correct path and plane structure to your golf swing, you have very little chance to play good golf. It doesn't matter if you have the most perfect grip, stance, rhythm, swing speed, posture, tempo, balance, length of swing, etc. If you don't swing the club back steep and down shallow in some degree, then you might as well take up bocci ball. Don't worry; I'll make it easy for you to establish this proper move.

Why Do We Slice?

Before I can talk about my system, I must first evaluate the situation you are currently in, to help you better comprehend what needs to be done to improve. I need you to understand why your current positions are so bad, to understand why the positions I will recommend shortly are so good.

Being fully aware of what state your golf game is in at the present moment is no different from any other situation you may face. In order to know how to get somewhere, you have to start by knowing where you are at the time. What is the first question someone asks you when you ask them for directions? *"Where are you?"*

As for the slicer, there are ultimately only two bad places that you can be in, because there are only two reasons why someone can slice the golf ball. There are no ifs, ands, or buts about it, it has to be one of the following:

1. **Over the Top**
2. **Open Clubface at Impact**

In spite of the fact that there are many indirect causes of each of these, which I will touch upon, the end result is always one of the previous two. I want you to become aware of the major pitfalls brought on by each of these, so you can better understand why the things that I suggest will help you.

Over the Top

The first and most common reason for slicing is from coming over the top. I refer to these slicers as Group 1 slicers because they represent about 90% of all slicers. Yes indeed, about nine out of every ten slicers you see roaming the course have this vicious move. This is also why my system that you will learn shortly is weighted heavily in the direction of the over-the-topper. The problem has been going on for too many years now, and I will go to any length to stop it.

Coming over the top is such a drastic problem that whoever has it would be much better off heading home, instead of going out to play. It's not just to spare themselves some humiliation. It's not just to keep the golf course in one piece. It's not just to speed up play. The reason those who have an over-the-top move should go home is because, quite simply, they have absolutely, positively, little chance to play decent golf.

The basic idea in coming over the top is...when you start your downswing, your arms move out away from your body and you swing above, or "over the top" of the ideal plane.

Over-the-Top Swing Sequence:

1. **Setup** - When golfers address the ball, they automatically establish their ideal swing plane. This will change slightly, depending on what club they are hitting.

2. **Backswing** - Over-the-top slicers will usually take the club back to the inside of this ideal plane. Even if they take it back on plane, trouble still awaits.

3. **Downswing** - The move after you reach the top of your swing is the most crucial one in all of golf. It is what they do at this point that causes people to be either low or high handicappers. Over-the-top

slicers will start this move by swinging their arms away from their body, and out above their ideal swing plane they had established at address. Low handicappers and pros will drop their arms to the correct inside position.

4. **Impact** - In order to get back to the ball to actually hit it, over-the-top slicers have to cut across the plane, thereby cutting across the ball. This produces the left-to-right spin on the ball—if the clubface is square or open—which ultimately sends it out slicing.

5. **Finish** - Who cares? The shot is already ruined.

• • •

There are many different reasons why you can place yourself into this over-the-top position. You have heard many of the phrases before, and I could give you a long list of things. Here are some of the more common:

- Sliding your head forward to start the downswing
- Opening your shoulders before impact
- Casting with your right arm and wrist
- Spinning out with your hips

All these things could very well result in putting you out over the proper swing plane, but what you need to understand is that no matter what the cause, the symptoms are always the same. By having your arms and golf club over the plane, you are forcing yourself to have to cut across the ball, which produces the left-to-right spin on it, which results in a nasty slice. It's that simple.

Because every instance results in one ultimate cutting-across action, I can conclude that one ultimate underneath move would fix everything. One ultimate underneath move of your *golf club*, that is, because, after all, it is your *golf club* that is going out over. It is your *golf club* that hits the ball. It is your *golf club* that creates the slice spin. If you can get that to stay inside, everything else will take care of itself.

Now certainly that may be easier said than done. After all, there are hundreds of "feels" and training products on the market that are designed to help cure these common over-the-top faults. There have been thousands of instructional pieces and lessons offered to help put an end to it. There have been countless hotel seminars and "legend-rich" documentaries crafted to aid you in overcoming your problem. You must think with all of this stuff that it is quite a complex task to get your club to come from the inside.

Guess what? It's not! Not if you use my Stick method, which I will get to in the next chapter. This drill will make it easy for you to come from the inside, or underneath the plane, which 99.9% of all great players do. As a result, you will bid farewell to your over-the-top swing path and be able to play a nice draw, a nice fade, or a nice straight shot. Stay tuned.

Open Clubface at Impact

The second reason for slicing is from having an open clubface at impact. I refer to these slicers as Group 2 slicers, because they represent only about 10% of the slicing population. Basically what this means is...somehow, this player is putting him or herself in a position where, at impact, their clubface is left wide open, which again produces the left-to-right spin, which results in a slice.

The players who fall into this category of slicer are, for the most part, pretty decent players. They usually have a good swing path and plane structure to their swing. As they usually have this most essential move already established, it becomes quite obvious that they do something wrong in their swing in terms of clubface positioning. (What else is there?)

The common mistakes this player makes:

1. Roll Face Open

The most common reason for an open clubface at impact is from an immediate rolling open of the club to start the swing. When this happens, the clubface is left

wide open at waist high (faces toward the sky), and left wide open at the top of the swing (toe points down). When you are put in this position at the top of your swing, it is virtually impossible to square the club up at impact. There must be a wild, compensating move made on the downswing, which will never be consistent.

2. Sharp Wrist Cock
A second common cause of an open clubface at impact is from a sharp, immediate wrist cock at the start of the

swing. When this happens, there is a large angle formed with the left wrist and forearm. This angle, sometimes referred to as the "dish angle," will also open up the clubface at the top of your swing. This again makes it quite difficult to square the club at impact. Another wild move must be made on the downswing to hit the ball on line.

3. Pull Heel Down

Players who suffer from this problem usually have a good clubface position at the top of their swing. It is close to the ideal position of having the clubface parallel with the left forearm. They are also the closest of the three open-clubface-at-impact slicer groups to hitting good shots. They make the mistake, however, of pulling the heel of the club so fiercely on the downswing that they end up wiping across the ball with an open clubface. They basically just hit it with a glancing blow. These players need some rotation of their arms through the shot. "Swinging the toe" is a good swing thought.

Too much "pull" leaves the clubface open.

For the most part, nothing too drastic must be changed within these three groups of players' swings to correct their slice. There are just some simple clubface positions that this type of slicer needs to better understand. I will never say to *not* pay attention to your path and plane, because these are the most important parts of the swing, but these players need to be especially wary of what their clubface is doing throughout the swing, and how it is manipulated.

As these players are, for the most part, good players, I believe that focusing on getting the clubface square at the three key points: waist high, top of swing, and, eventually, at impact, will greatly enhance the quality of their ball striking. It will take them from being good players, and turn them into excellent players. You will learn how that is done in a few minutes.

Over the Top vs. Open Clubface at Impact

There is some confusion in the world of golf as to what the main cause of the slice really is. I have just said that about 90% are over-the-top slicers, and about 10% are open-clubface-at-impact slicers, which I feel strongly to be true. Nonetheless, some of the top instructors in the world will tell you that the main cause of the slice is from an open clubface at impact. They will argue that every slice ever hit, including the ones hit by the players who swing over the top, was hit with this open clubface, and therefore slicers need to get some clubface rotation through the shot in order to stop it.

I was reading on the Internet recently where an excellent instructor from Florida, who happens to be one of the *Golf Digest* Top 100, was quoted as saying the following:

"Every slice ever hit was hit with an open clubface. This is the main reason for slicing. Slicers need to create more arm and hand rotation in order to stop it."

I agree with this person a bit, but I disagree with this person a lot. Maybe he's right. Maybe every single slice ever hit, including the over-the-top ones, was hit with an open clubface. It can happen with a square clubface, but for the purpose of discussion, let's say they all are hit with an open clubface.

Despite this, if you start telling golfers who swing the club over the top of the plane that the main cause of their slice is from an open clubface, and that they simply need to get some clubface rotation through the impact zone in order to stop it, *look out!* Those players will start hitting shots a hundred yards left of the target, or, worse yet, possibly through their own legs.

It is mentioned in this article that slicers need to get the sensation that they are "catching raindrops" on their follow through, like the one touring pro Hal Sutton has. I have this same reference on a videotape at home. In it, it is said that Hal would say he played his best golf when he felt like he could catch raindrops in the palm of his left hand when he got to waist high on the follow through.

Maybe Hal does have this feeling. Maybe he could catch raindrops, or hail, or floating cotton, or atmospheric dust, or falling stars, or space junk, or whatever. But Hal already has a superb shape to his golf swing. He is, in no way, an over-the-top slicer. Hal can afford the luxury of catching whatever he feels like in his left hand without the fear of removing his left ankle in the process. You, the over-the-top slicer, also need to get good shape to your swing before you can ever think of catching anything in your left hand.

Could you imagine swinging down from an angle that is so far out and above your ideal swing plane, and consciously trying to rotate the clubface through the hitting zone to the point where you can literally catch raindrops in the palm of your left hand? *Whoa!* You basically have two potential outcomes: You will either pull the ball far left of your target, or you will completely smother hook it right into the ground. You really have no other choices.

So all this clubface positioning, although it's a very important part of the swing, doesn't matter if you are still chopping at the ball from over the top. The shot will still turn out badly because of the direction in which you approached the ball.

The #1 cause of slicing and poor play in general is from coming over the top. *Encore!* The #1 cause of slicing and poor play in general is from coming over the top. The thing that good players do, that bad players don't, is swing the club steep, then shallow, which is the direct opposite of over the top. This is the move that you need to get in your swing before anything else, and when you are working on your game on the range, this is the move that must take precedence over any other aspect of the swing.

The problem is that most average players don't realize this. When I see high-handicap players out at the range hitting balls, it seems as though they don't care about path and plane a whole lot. They might line their clubs up on the ground just as they have read about or been told from someone. From there, they will most likely check their stance, posture, grip, and whatever else when preparing to hit the ball. Then, when they go to swing, they will hit a big over-the-top slice and wonder "...what went wrong?"

You have to get rid of your over-the-top path and plane structure before anything else matters in the golf swing. Once you can do this, and start swinging steep, then shallow, you may then fiddle around with other areas of the swing, including an important part such as clubface positioning.

• • •

If you want some verification that perhaps the most common trait among good players is swinging steep, then shallow, just look to the Tour. There are only two pros whom I can think of out there who don't do it, and, thus, have a legitimate over-the-top swing. One is Bruce Lietzke, and the other is Craig Parry. Granted, there are some players, such as Hale Irwin and Davis Love III, who tend to swing across the plane every now and then when they are going to play a fade. There are even some players, such as Ray Floyd and Nancy Lopez, who take the club way inside on the backswing, but stay underneath the plane on the downswing, and, consequently, do not slice. However, the only ones who do something comparable to what you would see at a public course are Lietzke and Parry.

Both of them take the club way inside going back, then swing way outside and across the ball coming down. They both play a huge cut, and as great as they are, that's all they can play. Even Bruce Lietzke says that there is no way he can hit anything other than a big fade. Even if he is on a sharp dogleg left, he will just play a mid-iron off the tee because he can't possibly draw the ball.

This is fine for Bruce. Bruce is great. And please understand that I love Bruce Lietzke. I think the fact that he plays only about ten tournaments a year, and still is competitive, is incredible. But the fact that every one other than he and Parry swings steep, then shallow, tells me, and it should probably tell you, that it is almost impossible to play good, consistent golf with an over-the-top swing, and it is 100% impossible to hit it straight.

• • •

It's this action of the best players in the world that has the most influence on my thought processes on the golf swing. I certainly don't put much credence in some scientists', physicists', or whacked-out ex-pros' explanation or attempt to conjure up the mechanically perfect swing, when not one single player on the PGA Tour is doing whatever they recommend.

This is also what I encourage from you. Check out the best golfers. See why they are so good. See how they swing the club. Watch for the inside move. Watch their body movements. Watch their heads. Watch their hips. Check out their divot patterns. Furthermore, if you see that they are not doing something, there is a good chance that you shouldn't be doing that, either.

When you see the Second Coming of Tiger Woods bend his left arm in a 90-degree angle at the top, you might want to become a believer. When you see the next Ernie Els attacking pins while swinging cross-handed, tell them to send more information. When you witness the next Justin Leonard finish on one foot and hop around a bunch of times, "convinced you shall becometh." Until then, your eyes will tell you everything you need to know.

Now, believe you me, there are plenty of goofy moves out there on the Tour. Just because certain players don't swing over the top doesn't mean that they don't look funny.

There are numerous great players who, at first view, may look like amateurs because of their strange stances, or tempos, or releases, or whatever (Paul Goydos and Allen Doyle, to name a couple). There are also great players whom you could mistake for being in your beer league on Tuesday afternoons (Tim Herron and Mark Carnevale come to mind). There are even some players whom you could mistake for Rogaine TV commercial candidates (Tom Lehman and Jim Furyk look the part). Rest assured, though, that all these players do what must be done in order to hit the ball well, what you will learn how to do quite easily, the three sweetest words in golf, and that's swing "steep, then shallow."

Steep, Then Shallow (Outside, Then Inside)

"What is all this steep, then shallow stuff anyway?" you might ask. "What the heck does it mean? How will it make my life any better?"

Well, it refers to the direction with which your club must travel throughout the swing. It must swing back steep, and come down shallow, in some degree. It can't travel the over-the-top way, which is back shallow, down steep.

"*WHAT?* Why so confusing, teacher? Why can't there be *one* plane in the swing? Why does there have to be this dual-plane, steep-then-shallow nonsense? Why can't I swing back 'stallow,' then down 'stallow'? Or why can't I swing back 'shalleep,' then down 'shalleep'? This would make things so much easier, wouldn't it?"

Unfortunately, because of the way we humans are constructed, it is almost impossible to swing on one plane throughout the entire swing. The way that our arm and leg joints act and react will automatically create more than one plane in the swing.

If you do try to swing on one plane, you have to basically wrap your arms around your body while your body stays dead still. This will close your clubface drastically, and you will have zero leverage with which to hit the ball. Your arms, wrists, legs, and hips will have no chance to move properly throughout the swing.

I have actually tried this one-plane stuff when I was in my *"Moe Norman worship stage."* This happened a short while after I was through with college and was searching precariously for some new swing method. It wasn't as intense a spell as the one before, yet it was still noticeable.

For all those who do not know of Moe, he is the legendary Canadian who is considered by many to be the best ball striker ever. It is also rumored that he swings on one plane throughout his swing. So I tried and tried to feel this one plane move to essentially copy Moe's swing. As I continued with it, the thought occurred to me, as I watched his videos and looked at some photos, that Moe doesn't swing on one plane during his whole swing.

Upon further review, Moe is excellent because he has a beautiful inside path into the ball, similar to other great ball strikers. His "top of swing" and "waist high on the downswing" positions look rather normal, square, and solid, if you ask me. Also, his post-impact release is not unlike what you would see out on the Tour these days. He just looks funny with that wide stance, that weird setup, and that even weirder finish (and those shoes!). One more thing about a one-plane swing: Iron Byron is just a machine.

THEREFORE, if you can't swing down on the same exact plane you swing back on, that leaves two options for you to choose from. You can either go *over* the plane, which I hope, by now, you realize is no good, or you can go *under* the plane, which is a move that is prevalent among pros, and, no doubt, the wise course of action.

Why this necessarily is, is something I am not qualified to answer. Call me stupid, but I certainly don't have much of a scientific explanation for why players need to swing the club down from the inside. I don't sit up every night measuring degrees and looking over charts to enhance my cerebral awareness of why, technically, good players must swing down from the inside. *I rescind in distinction to getting further multifarious in the calculable trivialities of said golf swing to be apt to render a metaphorical delineation as to why or what rung of optimal inside cusp of approximate verge upon works best.* I just know it has to be done because this is what the best players in the world do.

I'm also pretty confident that the easiest way to swing from the inside, when you have been an over-the-top slicer for so long, is if you make your backswing a little steeper (or a lot steeper in some cases). This will obviously create more of an inside path area for you to swing down on. It's difficult to create enough of an alleyway to come down from the inside if you also swing back to the inside. Some of the greats can do it, but for you, the over-the-top slicer, the more space you can get, the better off you will be.

CRUCIAL POINT: Before I can proceed, I need to make sure that you fully understand what's going on, and that you are not misinterpreting what it is that I am saying. You need to be aware that this notion of *steep, then shallow* is essentially the same thing as *outside, then inside.* That's why I put them both in the subtitle. Please don't mistake it to mean steep, as in "up and down." You never want to just pick your arms straight up on the takeaway. In fact, as I get into *The SELFish Four* shortly, you will see that I encourage a low, smooth, one-piece move away from the ball.

Instead, steep, then shallow simply refers to the fact that your golf club must travel back outside of where it comes down from, which again, is essentially the opposite of swinging over the top. That's basically it. There is nothing more to it than that, and nothing more that you need to concern yourself with at the present moment.

In technical terms, steep and shallow refer to the two planes you swing on, and outside and inside refer to the two paths you swing on. But this is not a technical book, so just remember that whenever I say "steep, then shallow," or "outside, then inside," I am, for all intents and purposes, referring to the same thing.

If it seems as though I am beating this steep-then-shallow point to death, it's because I am. If it seems that I am driving you nuts with this idea, then I have succeeded with what I have set out to do. I do not want to underestimate the importance of this move. As I said before, the thing that pros do that high-handicappers don't is that they swing the club back steep (outside), then down shallow (inside). It doesn't matter if you have the grip of Tiger Woods, the rhythm of Steve Elkington, the strength of Vijay Singh, and the mind of Jack Nicklaus. If you don't have the proper moves regarding swing path and plane, you can forget about playing good golf.

It is also important to note that this steep-then-shallow move is relative to all players' swings. For instance, Ben

Hogan had a flat backswing, but he still swung steep, then shallow, because his downswing was more shallow than his backswing. You could probably say Hogan swung flat, then flatter.

This, incidentally, is why many golfers have trouble when they read *Five Lessons: The Modern Fundamentals of Golf.* For as great a book as it is, it spells doom for most slicers when they pick it up. Mr. Hogan talks about swinging back underneath a pane of glass. This is a good feel for a great player such as Ben, who already had a pure downswing move to begin with, but when over-the-top slicers try to swing back underneath this glass, which *will* flatten out their backswing, they have no chance. All this will do is encourage an even bigger over-the-top move to get back to the ball.

MEMO TO ALL OVER-THE-TOP SLICERS… Please do not think of this pane of glass on your backswing. You need to think steep (outside) on your backswing. Once you have established an inside swing path on your downswing, you may then entertain the thought of this glass to possibly tighten up your swing. Until then, break the glass!

On the other side of things, you have Jack Nicklaus. Jack's swing is more "up the line, down the line" than most players are. Even though Jack has a bit of a steeper angle of attack than Hogan and some other greats, his downswing is still inside relative to his backswing. Something tells me that this is why he is great. This is also the reason that his typical shot throughout his career was a fade.

Jack's move also ties into the fact that some players are more exaggerated with this steep-then-shallow move than others. Players such as Nick Price and Lee Trevino have an obvious shallowing of the plane to start their downswing. Lee has that big loop in his swing, resembling a figure 8.

Nick has that really cool shallowing out move to start his downswing. It's poetry in motion, for sure. (By the way, I think Nick Price's swing plane is a model for every over-the-top slicer in the world to emulate.)

Other players, including Greg Norman and Tiger Woods, swing a little more on the same plane throughout their entire swings. Tiger's swing, especially his practice swing, may give you the illusion that he comes over the top. Don't be fooled because he as well swings outside, then inside. He just has that immediate straightening of the right arm on the downswing, which creates less of a gap between his forearms halfway down, and thus, less of an inside move. Still, it's from the inside relative to his backswing. It would be impossible for him to hit it right to left if he came over the top.

Greg's positions are excellent as well. For someone who swings hard, he is very mechanically sound. He just might have the best "right elbow to hip" connection halfway down that I have ever seen. This creates what I like

to call "The Magic Gap." *Check out that gap between his forearms. Is that not sweet?* Greg's right elbow connects, and the gap is formed. This sets him on a beautiful inside path from where he can attack the ball. From that position, he has almost no chance of hitting a bad shot.

Something else that is fun to do, now that you understand this path and plane structure, is to track down the Tour players who really have this nice outside-then-inside, steep-then-shallow swing. You can learn a lot from them by studying their swing shape and trying to incorporate some of what you see into your swing. Look to players such as Ernie Els *(see page 88)*, Nick Price *(see page 89)*, Colin Montgomerie *(see page 90)*, Tom Watson *(see page 91)*, Fred Couples, and Jay Don Blake. All of them set the club quite outside and steep going back, then bring it down from the inside so pure. For lefties, take a look at a newcomer to the Tour, Steve Flesch. He may not be a household name just yet, but the guy has a strong game. More importantly, he has a beautiful steep-then-shallow swing, from which you can learn a great deal.

Certainly, you don't have to be as exaggerated as these players are with your own swing path and plane. However, when you have been doing something completely wrong time after time, such as swinging over the top, the idea is to do just the opposite. It's better to look at a Freddie Couples, who takes the club way steep, then turns and reroutes massively to the inside, than it would be to study a Davis Love III, who has less of a degree of difference between his backswing and downswing planes.

Another player to whom slicers should really pay particular attention is Jim Furyk. I know some of you cringe when you see him swing. I know some of you would rather have a root canal than to watch him strike a ball. The fact is that slicers, and all other golfers for that matter, can learn a great deal from his swing. He does some things from a mechanical standpoint that should be emulated by all of us.

His swing plane is obviously super steep going back. He then drops it to the inside very nicely coming down. Dare I say it reminds me of Nick Faldo's swing? *O.K. Maybe it doesn't!* But even with a rather gangly action, Jim is a great player because he has an excellent path and plane structure to his swing. This results in an impact position that's as solid as anyone in the world. So who cares if his swing is a 2-second horror flick? Who cares if you may need a sick bag in order to watch him pound balls? The guy does what needs to be done to hit the ball well, and that's why he is great.

The Bottom Line...

The point with all this discussion is that if Jim, Greg, Tiger, Freddie, or any other good player swung over the top, they would be lucky to be club pros, much less champions. (just don't tell Lietzke or Parry that).

On the following pages are photographs of four world-class players. Notice the difference in their backswing and downswing planes. Each of them swings relatively steep (outside) on the way back, and shallow (inside) on the way down. This swing structure is the most crucial part of the golf swing.

Ernie Els

Nick Price

Colin Montgomerie

Tom Watson

▸ 5 ◂

"Now this is not the end. It is not even the beginning of the end.
But it is perhaps, the end of the beginning."
—*Sir Winston Churchill*

The SELFish Four

*N*o matter what type of slicer you are—over the top or open clubface at impact—you will find help with the *noslice.com* four-part model system. This is the system that I have spent years developing. I have gone to painstaking depths to come up with something that could eliminate even the most severe slice. I, personally, hit countless slices before I figured out how to correct it with this very simple system.

My system, referred to as *The SELFish Four*, consists of the following:

1. **S**tick
2. **E**xtend
3. **L**ook
4. **F**igure

If you put these four together, what you get is an acronym for SELF. It is one of my goals to make you become more SELFish with your golf game, SELFish in respect to using my approach, and selfish in respect to trusting yourself with the knowledge I provide you. Focus on the essentials of the golf swing, which are covered in this four-part model, and trust yourself in getting better.

• • •

As I get started, let me ask a question that you may have on your mind, and that is the following:

What exactly am I trying to accomplish with The SELFish Four?

Well, because I know that there are only two reasons why someone can slice the ball, it becomes quite apparent that I would look to those areas and try to correct them. I know that 10% of slicers are open-clubface-at-impact slicers, so I have devoted one of the parts of my model to getting your clubface in a square position. I know that 90% of slicers are over-the-top slicers, so I have devoted most everything else to getting rid of that. Therefore, for good reason, I am heavily weighted to the side of getting rid of your over-the-top move, and getting the more conventional steep-then-shallow move, which is the most important part of the swing.

That said, the first two, *Stick* and *Extend*, should be used by over-the-top slicers. The third one, *Look*, should be used by open-clubface-at-impact slicers. The last one, *Figure*, can be used by either type of slicer. *SELF on!*

STICK

Of all the approaches to fixing the golf swing, Stick, in my opinion, is the best one that the over-the-top slicer will ever find to teach him or herself the correct mechanics in the swing. The name stick comes from the fact that I use about a two-to-three-foot-long dowel stick to do this drill.

There are three methods that I use the stick for and certain variations within each method.

The three methods are as follows:
1. Outside, Inside
2. Gap
3. Ground

Outside, Inside

This might be the greatest drill of all time. At least I think so. If there is ever a drill that will get you to do this steep, then shallow; outside, then inside stuff that I have emphasized so far, it is this one.

The popular form of this drill over the years has been to place a broken shaft in the ground in a stationary, vertical position. From there, you would swing outside the shaft on the way back, then inside the shaft on the way down. I know from personal experience, this works really well. It certainly gets you to better understand the correct path and plane you need in your swing.

However, I have improved upon this drill by exploring its versatility. I realized that much more could be done with this drill than merely sticking a broken shaft in the ground in a vertical position. I noticed that simply changing the position of the shaft (or stick), and the angle it is set on, could produce a different type of shot altogether, such as a slight fade or a huge hook, all while having the correct mechanics in the swing. All the successes I've had from these experiments have led me to conclude that this is perhaps *the* greatest drill, and swing thought, in the history of golf.

The Outside, Inside drill works as follows:

Step 1 – Put a stick in the ground about 1-4 feet outside your right foot.

Step 2 – Put it halfway between the ball-target line and your toe line, and on a slight angle.

Step 3 – Swing outside the stick on the way back.

Step 4 – Swing inside the stick on the way down.

If you swing outside the stick, then inside the stick, everything else will take care of itself. All the swing thoughts and quick tips you may have read about in books over the years to help stop a slice will seem to happen automatically, without your having to be totally conscious of them.

Step 3.

Step 4.

These are things such as:

- ✓ tuck your right elbow into your pocket
- ✓ hold your back to the target
- ✓ rotate your shoulders underneath
- ✓ keep your head behind the ball
- ✓ bump your hips laterally
- ✓ keep your left shoulder high
- ✓ hold your right shoulder stationary
- ✓ point the handle of the club at the ball
- ✓ create a gap between your forearms

That's not all this wonderful drill accomplishes, mind you. It doesn't just create the proper *anti-slice* positions that you need to be in, but it also produces other good moves within the swing, such as the weight shift and the wrist cock, without much effort.

You can witness how these important moves will be incorporated into your swing by taking a face-on view of your swing while doing this drill. When you swing back outside the stick, notice that slight weight shift into the inside of your right leg. This is a key move that you need in your swing, but one you should never be conscious of making. It should happen naturally, and it will if you simply swing outside the stick. If you focus on making this weight shift, it will most likely turn into a sway, which is bad. If you start rocking the boat too much, you know what will happen.

Also notice how a little hinging and unhinging of your wrists will take place. I certainly don't want you to *think* of making a wrist cock. This is another move in the golf swing that should happen naturally. If you concentrate on cocking your wrists, you will most likely set them too early or too much, and, as a result, leave your clubface wide open or totally closed.

• • •

The main reason why I love the Outside, Inside drill so much is because it teaches the over-the-top slicer the swing structure that 99.9% of pros on the PGA Tour use. This involves a steep backswing plane and a shallow downswing plane. This drill gives this particular slicer the opportunity to feel—although in an exaggerated way—this correct move in the most simple means possible.

Most slicers have never been able to feel this correct sensation. Even if they have tried some "anti-slice feels" in their swings, they will most likely still throw the club over the top, because their brains and bodies have been so conditioned to do it that way. Nothing has prevented them from making these nasty moves. But not with the stick. It will guide you into the correct positions you need to be in, and stop you from the disastrous whipping of the club way to the inside going back.

Outside, Inside FAQ's
Q. What type of stick do I use?

A. In the pictures shown, I use a simple dowel stick, about 2.5-feet long. You can use pretty much anything that is somewhat thin and which you can stick in the ground. It's also a good idea to use something that is easy to stick in and out of the ground, so it makes it less of a hassle to change the position of the stick. You have to move around sometimes to avoid hitting shots out of divots.

Furthermore, it may be quite helpful if you use a stick that is colorful. This may make it optically appear that the stick is still there when you are out playing and not permitted to use it. I remember when I was first doing this drill how I would paint different patterns on the stick. I would whip out the Krylon and start putting red and yellow spots all over it. I wanted to have this stick represent not only a physical aid, but a visual aid as well. The use of color certainly helped. I was able to recognize the stick easily and this, in turn, allowed me to use it as a "swing thought" on the course, where it worked wonders. *It is, quite simply, the greatest swing thought ever!* I could just set up to the ball, imagine the stick was there, and rip the ball while swinging outside it, then inside it. As for the stick color, though, don't stress this too much. For now, just get something you can stick in the ground.

Q. How much of an angle and how far away do I set the stick?

A. This will change, depending on which club you are hitting. The basic idea of setting the stick on an angle is so you can have a smoother, more one-piece takeaway. If the stick is too vertical and stands too tall, it may force you to lift your arms to clear it, which is not a good move at all. If you are using a driver or long irons, angle it more away from you. This will help with such a long club. For shorter clubs, less of an angle is fine.

As for placement, make sure you give yourself plenty of space. This is key. The farther away, the easier it is. For long irons and woods, set it a considerable distance away because you have a longer arc with those clubs. For short irons and wedges, a little closer is fine because those clubs don't require as much space.

Longer clubs.

Shorter clubs.

Important: It's significant to note that the angle you set the stick on, and the positioning of it in relation to your right foot, are not necessarily "set in stone." I am going to leave that up to you and what you feel most comfortable with through your own experimenting with this drill. Everyone is different and I understand that. Some people have even told me that they set the stick outside of where they swing, and just use it on a peripheral basis, because it's too hard for them to physically swing around it. (Or they will just imagine the stick is there and use it as a swing thought.) Because it can be difficult for some is why I allow for flexibility with regard to this drill.

What I am not flexible on, and what *is* set in stone, is that you swing outside the stick on the way back, then inside it on the way down. If you don't do that, then this drill will not be very effective. So to be sure that you make this happen, place the stick enough in the middle of your ball-target line and toe line, and give yourself enough space. This will instill in you the added confidence you need to swing outside, then inside.

It's also a good idea to take a lot of practice swings going outside, then inside to get this steep-then-shallow feeling down. You don't want to just grab a bucket of balls and start ripping away. Practice until you feel comfortable with it, then you can start hitting some shots.

Neat Stick Tips...
What is so sweet about this Outside, Inside stick drill is that you, the over-the-top slicer, can practice just about any shot you would like to play, and still have the correct steep-then-shallow mechanics you need.

For instance, if you want to play a fade, place the stick out away from your right foot, more on the ball-target line.

You still swing outside it on the way back, then inside it on the way down. Because the stick was placed so far away from you, you will be cutting across the ball enough on the downswing to produce a little left-to-right spin, which produces a fade.

Frank Nobilo and Mark Calcavecchia are a couple of

players on the Tour who fit this shape of swinger quite nicely. If you ever get a chance to see them play, notice *how* they play their fade. They sure as heck don't loop the club way inside going back, then hack over the top to play a fade. Instead, they take the club steep and outside, then drop it on top of the ball while swinging down the line. They both have the correct mechanics in their swing that keeps that fade from turning into a wicked slice.

On the other hand, if you want to play a power hook, place the stick closer to your right foot, and also on more of a vertical angle if you choose *(next page)*. When you do this, it forces you to come way from the inside in order to miss the stick. As a result of coming way from the inside like this, you will produce a lot of right-to-left spin on the ball, which will create that large draw.

Mark Brooks, when he is playing well, is someone on the Tour who would represent this type of swinger. He loves playing that huge draw. As you can see, at least at the 1996 PGA Championship, which he won at Valhalla, he brings it way from the inside. He just sets his club in a rather normal position at the top, then reroutes it severely to the inside. You could almost stand behind him and envision him swinging around a stick.

Keep in mind, though, that these "hook and fade" stick positions are extremes. Be sure to practice them only after you have been using the stick in its normal position. Don't get too crazy at first. This drill is going to feel awkward enough for you the first time you do it because of your habit of coming over the top. What you will be doing now is just the opposite of what you have been doing for years.

Also keep in mind that these stick positions are primarily for an *over the topper* who wants to play these particular shots. They are not necessarily for a player who

has good path and plane fundamentals. For those players, playing different types of shots is just a matter of opening or closing their body angles. From there, everything else would fall into place. For over-the-top players, it is not quite that simple. They need to get that outside, then inside swing structure grooved in every situation, and that is what the Stick drill will cause to happen.

● ● ●

So please work on this Outside, Inside drill religiously. It's one of the best things ever for the over-the-top slicer. Not only is it easy to understand, but it doesn't take long for someone to catch on to it. When I first started to do this drill, I was hitting good shots within 5-10 balls, and this was with a completely different swing than I was using for the previous million or so shots.

This drill also taught me the correct positions in a very natural way. It kept my sequence of motion, and things such as my tempo and swing length, intact throughout. It's not something that inhibited me as do many training aids that are on the market today. No, it did not call for me to strap my arms to my body so tightly that it would cut off the circulation. It did not make me put some clicking instrument on my wrist that is extremely annoying. It even avoided the complementary use of some crazy contraption on my right knee that would have made me look like robo-pro. *More unlike these things, the Stick drill worked!*

Every slicer on the globe who has bought some of these "aids" should throw them away and do the following: Get a stick. Put it in the ground. Swing outside it on the way back, inside it on the way down, and let everything else take care of itself.

Gap

This is another great drill that you can do with your trusty stick. It places less emphasis on the backswing, but really creates that shallow approach into the ball you need. Because it is less backswing intensive, I recommend you do this after the Outside, Inside drill. As you now know, one of the major factors in swinging over the top is from whipping the club too far to the inside going back. You need to get the club moving outside on the backswing, first and foremost.

The Gap drill works as follows:

Step 1 – Place the stick on the other side of the ball from where you set up. Set it on an angle that closely resembles your shaft angle. Leave a gap of 6-12 inches between the ball and the stick.

Step 2 – Set up. Swing.

Swing the club back in its normal position, then hit the ball while missing the stick, obviously. The stick, positioned where it is, will prevent you from throwing your right side out, over the top. If you did, you would smack into the stick. *Yikes!*

This drill is going to be scary at first. I can almost guarantee that you will be a little fearful to begin. Because of this, it's important to leave a large enough gap when you first do it. Somewhere around 8-12 inches is fine for starters. You can also set the stick on more of a vertical angle as another way of easing your way into this drill.

The first time I did this I was hitting shots way off the toe because I was afraid I would smack into the stick. I had been opening up my shoulders drastically before impact, and I knew if I did that while doing this drill, I might be picking splinters out of the right side of my body.

Don't worry; if it feels strange, and you are a little scared, that probably means that you are doing it correctly. Just don't be so intimidated that you end up never trying it. This drill provides an excellent sensation of keeping your right shoulder back, which will lead to some well-struck shots. Your right shoulder should feel as though it "stays put" when you start your downswing. You may have even seen some instructors stand behind or in front of a player and put their club on the player's back shoulder. This is to keep it from throwing out. This is what Michigan pro Ron Beurmann did with me, and it definitely taught me the proper shoulder move on the downswing.

Ground

This drill is fairly similar to the Gap method. They both encourage a shallow downswing by keeping your right shoulder stationary when you start your move down. But the Ground drill gives a different look. It is certainly a lot less intimidating look, which may be a benefit to some players. This drill will really help you to produce those shallow divots you see the Tour pros take. Say bye-bye to those huge, chunky, pork-chop-sized pieces of turf, which point straight left.

The Ground drill works as follows:

Step 1 – Lay the stick on the ground about 3-6 inches to the right side of the ball. Line it up parallel to where you are aiming.

Step 2 – Set up. Swing.

Once again, the stick positioned where it is will prevent you from going over the top. If you did, you would smack into the stick, and you might break it in half, or at least be tentative coming into impact. To prevent this, be sure to leave enough space when you first do this drill, just as in the Gap method. The last thing you want to be is afraid. You need to gradually work your way into this one as well.

Something else that is neat about the Ground drill is how it will help you to line your clubface up with the target. Remember when you are setting the stick on the ground, to do so in a parallel direction to the target line. This will get your clubface, which is the most important thing to get lined up correctly, in the proper position to hit the ball. It is quite helpful.

Stick Conclusion

I bet you never thought a simple stick could help your game so much, but it definitely can. As I just showed you, there are three drills in one that you can do with Stick. Outside, Inside is the one you should practice first. You need to get rid of your over-the-top move, *period.* The best way to do this is to create a feel that will get you to do the opposite. Swinging outside the stick on the way back, then inside it on the way down, will do just that.

From there, go on to the Gap and Ground methods. These are more downswing intensive, and will make your swing more shallow through impact. They both do pretty much the same thing, but each represents a different look and feel. As a result, you may prefer one of them over the other. That is fine, that is all right, but be sure to keep them both in mind, work on them regularly, and start developing the proper inside move into the ball.

EXTEND

The Extend method is also great for the over-the-top slicer. It is basically just an "extension" of the Stick approach. In both cases, what I am ultimately trying to get you to do is get rid of your *inside, looping, out, over, hacking motion,* and get the more appropriate steep-then-underneath move.

However, Extend accomplishes this more with the lower body. It gets your lower body to react properly throughout the shot to put you in a powerful, underneath position at impact. By doing so, it will prevent a common cause of coming over the top, which is from clearing your hips too early on the downswing. This means that the hips abruptly turn out of the way, instead of first shifting laterally. This causes loss of distance and oftentimes wicked slices. Extend will correct these problems by getting your hips to fire laterally enough to start the downswing.

If you look at the great ball strikers in the world, you will see that this is what they do. They all bump their hips forward, then turn them out of the way. This bump is what you need to do in your swing, and this bump is what you will learn in Extend. So once you have learned the correct upper-body mechanics, which Stick teaches, you are now ready to incorporate your lower body, as well as add power to your swing, with Extend.

The Extend drill works as follows:

Step 1 – Lay two flat objects on the ground: one going straight away from you on the ball-target line, and the other out ahead of you, on about a 20-30 degree angle away from the ball-target line.

Step 2 – Set up. Swing straight back along the first piece.

Step 3 – Bump your lower body along the second piece
to start things down. This will drop everything
(arms, shoulders, and elbows) into the slot. It
should momentarily make it feel as though you are
swinging out to right field.

Step 4 – Once you have this sensation, or bump to the
right, you may then clear your hips out of the way
and fire through the ball as hard as you want. *Fire
through hard!* Once you get everything in the slot,
you are free to rip away without fear of going over
the top.

Note: You do not want to swing along the second angle
for your entire downswing. If you did that, then you would
obviously hit a wild shot to the right. The piece of wood is
set on that angle to remind you that you need to get just the
initial movement in that direction. Also, do not think of this

drill in step-by-step fashion. I have it listed this way to better illustrate the point, but the entire motion of your lower body is a flowing, as well as an aggressive, reaction.

• • •

I think the two best players on the Tour to look at in terms of this motion are Nick Faldo and Tiger Woods. They both swing relatively straight back to load up on the inside of their right leg. From there, Tiger certainly has more rotational speed than Nick, but the mechanics of their lower body on the downswing are very similar. Both of them have a little lateral movement starting down, *then* clear their hips out of the way. This lateral shift is key. It results in everything dropping perfectly into the slot. At that point, they can fire as hard as they want at the ball and hit good shots.

This motion is also important for generating distance. When you swing straight back along the first piece of wood, this will build tension on the inside of your right leg. You will have a lot of "stored up" energy there. When you swing down along the second piece, your lower body will automatically fire because your area of least resistance is in front of you. Consequently, all of that "stored" lower body energy will be released through the ball.

• • •

In addition to this, and perhaps more important, is how this correct lower-body motion forms a bow position at impact with the right side of the body. This signifies that players have shifted their hips, then turned them out of the way, all while keeping their upper body back. If there is ever something in addition to the correct swing path and plane that you will see in common with great players, it is this move. It is this *upper body back, lower body forward,* concave bow with the right side of their body at impact.

Keep this image in mind for your swing. Check to see if you can achieve this position. Videotape your swing, and notice where your body is at impact. If the left side of your body appears too straight up and down, this means that your upper body has gone too far forward, or your lower body has hung back too much, but if you see that bow, your scores could be going low *(next page)*.

Another player you might want to watch with regard to this lower-body move is Nick Price. When Nick gets into trouble with his swing it is because he has too much of a lateral move with his hips. This forces him to come too far from the inside, and thus, he starts to hit shots off line. This should also tell you, the slicer, that the side to err on with regard to the lower body on the downswing is to have it go

"The Bow."

laterally too much. You want to avoid, at all costs, that quick spin-out move with the hips that will cause you to throw your right side over the top. *You gotta' get the bump.*

Extend FAQ's
Q. What type of objects do I use for this drill?

A. For right now, use any two relatively flat objects you would like. Golf clubs will work fine. In my photos, I use two pieces of wood. This is more for the camera than anything. I want to make sure that you can clearly see and understand what I am doing.

Q. How much of an angle do I set the second piece on?

A. In the photos I have, it is set on approximately a 30-degree angle. This is about standard. Any comparable angle, give or take a few degrees, will be fine.

Although, when you are first doing this drill, it's a good idea to take some practice swings with it set on a fairly large angle. Get the feeling that you are bumping way to the right of the target. This will groove, much more substantially, the lower-body shift and dropping of the club to the inside that you need to get established in your swing.

You can also hit different types of shots with this second piece set on more or less than a 30-degree angle. If you want to play a huge hook, set it on a huge angle. You still swing straight back along the first piece to load up on the inside of your right leg, then bump everything along that second piece. This large bump to the right will force you to come way from the inside. Once you clear your hips and release, an abundance of right-to-left spin will be created on the ball, which will result in a large hook.

If you want to play a shot with less sidespin, place it on more of a straight-down-the-line angle. This will make your bump more laterally straight, instead of laterally right. As a result, your club will not be rerouted as much to the inside, so you will produce less hookspin. *Experiment!*

Similar to the Stick method, you have to work your way into this drill at an easy pace. Don't get too liberal with the placement of the second piece of wood to start. Set it on an angle you feel comfortable with. The whole idea is to get the initial move of your lower body going laterally and to the right, so you avoid clearing too early and throwing everything over the top. How far right that is will depend on how comfortable you feel and what you are trying to accomplish with this drill. The only thing that matters is you do it in some degree, avoid the spin out of the hips, and get the club swinging from a powerful, inside position.

LOOK

I use the Look method for the 10% of slicers who are open-clubface-at-impact slicers. Although there are not many of you who hit a slice from solely having an open clubface at impact, those who do must also be considered. Those of you who slice from doing both things wrong— over the top and open clubface at impact—will also want to pay particular attention to this drill.

The basic idea of this drill is to get your clubface *"looking"* at the ball at waist high, so it can be square there, square at the top of your swing, and square again at impact. There is no prop needed to do this drill.

The Look drill works as follows:

Step 1 – Set up to the ball.
Step 2 – Swing back to waist high while keeping your clubface *"looking"* at the ball *(next page)*. Continue on and hit the shot.

Do this drill a few times until it feels natural. It will probably feel as though the clubface is closed to you at waist level, but it is most likely square. This is because you are so used to having your clubface facing the sky (wide open) at waist level. If you can get it in this square position, the chances are good that it will remain square throughout the rest of your swing.

What I don't want you to do, however, is to shut down the face of your club at waist level *(pg. 122)*. This will cause you to be in an extremely closed position at the top of your swing with your clubface facing the sky. This may lead to some other problems, which will require many more

Square.

Closed.

compensations to be made in order to achieve square contact. (It could even lead to some embarrassment, as your playing partners might think that you're busing tables or serving cocktails with that top-of-swing position!)

So make sure your clubface is as square as possible. A good way to check to see if it's square is to set your club down once it gets to waist level. If it resembles your spine angle, it's square. If the toe is way ahead of the heel, it's shut. If the heel is ahead of the toe, you have rolled the face open. Adjust accordingly when presented with those situations.

• • •

If you get a chance to study some of the pros' swings, notice their clubface position at the *top*. This is usually an indication of what has happened in their takeaway. It will also give you an idea of what they will have to do on the downswing in order to hit a good shot.

If players are in the ideal position at the top of having the clubface parallel with their left forearm, then they have kept the clubface square and looking at the ball on the takeaway. From this good position, they are ready to go after the ball hard and play a fade, a draw, or hit it straight. Players whose clubfaces are closed at the top, with the clubface facing the sky, have shut the face down for the first three feet away from the ball. Consequently, they have to rotate their body open quite a bit in order to square the club at impact. They must hang on for dear life upon making contact. Those whose clubfaces are open at the top, and "hang the toe," have rolled open the clubface in the first three feet of the swing. Thus, they generally need to rotate their hands and arms a great deal through the impact zone. This is inconsistent at best. All of these top-of-swing positions can be related to the takeaway.

If you are looking for a Tour player who has as good a takeaway as anyone, watch Greg Norman. He has some of the best clubface positions you will ever see. There is no rolling-open action of the clubface in Greg's swing. Nor is there any hooding. It's square at waist high, and square at the top. He doesn't need to make any drastic compensation on the downswing to allow for him to be aggressive through the shot.

Check grip...possibly

This is the only part of my teaching model where I mention anything about the grip. Usually I don't dwell on the grip, because let's face it, with all the different grips out there, who is to say which one is correct? Also, with all the different human feel characteristics, who is to say which grip is best suited for whom?

However, it's important to note that the grip does have an effect on clubface positions, and can be related to whether or not a golfer will slice the ball. If your grip is too weak, with your hands turned too far to the left, you will have the tendency to leave your clubface open throughout the swing. This, quite obviously, is what open-clubface-at-impact slicers usually have trouble with. From this weak grip, they will likely roll the club open during the first three feet of the backswing. Unless they hold their arms quite rigid, they have almost no choice but to rotate clockwise, which opens up the clubface. This is a bad move!

If you do this, then what you need to do is to strengthen your grip by turning your hands to the right and more

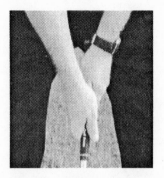

Weak.

Strong.

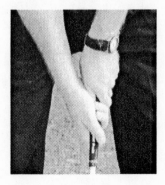

Too strong.

underneath the club. The "V's" formed by the thumb and forefinger should be pointing somewhere around your right shoulder. This will make it much easier for you to keep your clubface square, and will significantly decrease that rolling-open sensation. Be sure, however, not to overcompensate and make your grip too strong; with your hands turned too far to the right, and way underneath the club. This will cause your clubface to be closed throughout the swing and may turn your slice into a snap hook.

Please keep in mind that if you absolutely cannot do this, or a slight change in your grip will throw your entire natural motion out of sync, then by all means don't do it. I would much rather see you compensate in some other area of the swing that is not such a "feel" aspect. I realize that if you can't be comfortable before you hit the shot, how in the world will you be comfortable during it?

Still, what should be encouraging to those who I would like to see make a little change, is that nearly every good player on the PGA Tour has some form of a strong grip. Regardless if they have an overlap (Vardon), interlock, or ten-finger grip—which, by the way, are all perfectly fine— most have their hands turned to the right with the "V's" pointing somewhere around their right shoulder. This gives them so much more leverage in the swing and the ability to have that powerful, late release.

Once again, the Tour tells the tale! The players out there are the ones to look at, and the players out there happen to do the exact opposite of the two main causes of a slice. Nearly every one swings steep, then shallow, and nearly every one has some form of a strong grip.

This strong grip is a characteristic of the longer hitters as well. Take Tiger Woods, for instance. He offers a perfect example of a strong left hand. This gives him late-release power, on top of the power he gets from amazing hip speed. (No wonder he is so long a hitter.) If it's good enough for Tiger Woods, then chances are that it will be good enough for you, too.

By taking these two facts into account...

- Weak grip = open clubface
- Most good players have a strong grip

...I conclude that the open-clubface-at-impact slicer would be better off with a slightly stronger grip.

• • •

Just remember; the essence of this, the third part of *The SELFish Four*, is that your clubface "looks" at the ball, not the sky, at waist high.

FIGURE

The Figure method can be used by either the over-the-top slicer, or the open-clubface-at-impact slicer. The term Figure is short for *Figure 89*, and that is what I want the shape of your swing to be in: in the shape of a figure 8 on the backswing, and a figure 9 on the downswing. You will need one of the objects used in the Extend method.

The Figure drill works as follows:

Step 1 – Place the object on the ground behind the ball on about a 30-degree angle. This represents the "leg" of the number 9.

Step 2 – Set up to the ball.

Step 3 – Swing back in the shape of a figure 8.

Step 4 – Swing down along the leg of the number 9.

Step 4.

The backswing figure 8 will keep your clubface square to waist level, and will also put you on the correct steep (outside) swing plane. The downswing figure 9 will reroute the club to the correct shallow (inside) position, and will also get your lower body to fire as you swing down along the leg of the number nine. So this *Figure 89* drill basically just encompasses everything that I have talked about up to this point. Stick, Extend, and Look can all be found within it.

Make no mistake; its main intention, as is rather apparent with its shape, is to help get rid of your over-the-top swing. It has a bit of a different look and feel to it than Stick and Extend, but its purpose is pretty much the same. You want the end result to be an elimination of an over-the-top swing path, and the use of a powerful, inside move into the ball.

Regarding this inside move, remember *how* it should be achieved. Be sure to do it just the way I show you; that is, having something there to represent the leg of the number nine, such as the piece of wood shown. It will keep your mind aware that you must come down on that angle. Without it, you might have the tendency to throw your right side over the top, because your brain has not yet been trained to swing down from the inside. It still needs to be told.

Something else that you can do to reinforce this inside move is to imagine the golf ball is divided into four quadrants. Picture the leg of the number nine pointing directly at the back-left quadrant. Then try to hit that part of the golf ball while swinging down along the leg. This thought adds a little more emphasis to this drill, which may be just what you need.

Figure FAQ's

Q. "Do I have to use a piece of wood, or may I use a golf club instead?"

A. A golf club is okay for this drill, but it's not the best. When doing something such as this, the flatter the object lies to the ground, the better off you will be. If you don't have a piece of wood, find something else that is flat. Heck, tape some paper together and use that, as long as the wind doesn't blow it away, or make a line with a can of paint, as long as the greens superintendent is not around. Just get something that is flat to help reinforce the inside move into the ball.

Q. "May I change the angle of the 'leg'?"

A. Yes, you may. The angle is simply there as a reference point. How much or how little an angle you set it on will depend on what you are most comfortable with.

Also, in relation to how you place the "leg," it's a good idea to leave a large enough gap between the golf ball and the object you use. You don't want to be scared and think you will smack into whatever you put there. If you are worried about making contact with the object, you will be very tentative coming into impact, and more than likely come out of the shot and hit it thin. So leave yourself plenty of space.

• • •

This "89" shape could also make it feel as though you are swinging like Lee Trevino, with that exaggerated outside-inside loopy move of his. But this is the feeling you want to have. All your years of coming inside-then-over-the-top will probably make this move feel awkward to you, but this is actually good. You want the complete opposite sensation that you had with your over-the-top swing, and that is what this drill will give you.

Notice how the club comes out of Lee's head on the backswing, and just above his waist on the downswing. An amazing rerouting of the club to the inside.

A good thing to remember to do, in an all-out fight against this over-the-top swing, is to practice this type of drill at home. Stand up in your living room if you are watching television or something, and start doing some figure 8 type circles with your arms and shoulders. You do not need a golf club to do it. Just stand up and make a series of reverse over-the-top motions. You will notice that doing things such as this will greatly reduce the time it takes to get rid of your slice.

Don't worry if it feels funny, or if you feel that you look funny by doing it. Anything to get rid of your over-the-top swing path should be your #1 priority. It is the worst move in the swing and it has to be done away with before you can become a good player. So whether you are at home, at work, or at the golf course, as long as you are making some steep-then-shallow movements, which this Figure 89 drill teaches, you will be making progress toward being a consistently straight and powerful hitter.

Conclusion

The slice is a problem that has plagued golfers for many years, but it is not that difficult to correct, as long as you focus on what is necessary in the golf swing. Most necessary of all is this outside-then-inside; steep-then-shallow swing path and plane structure, which you will find with just about every great player who has ever played the game..

This most essential of moves is what I focused heavily on in *The SELFish Four* teaching model. I realize that if you want to become a good player, you cannot have an over-the-top swing. History, statistics, and common sense will tell you that you basically have no chance of playing good golf while swinging over the top. You must instead come from the inside, just as 99.9% of the players on the Tour do.

● ● ●

Work, work, work on these drills to get rid of your slice. Every slicer can improve significantly from this SELFish Four method. Just as importantly, be aware of certain aspects of the swing that you do not need to concern yourself with. Such meaningless attention to these details will prevent you from focusing on what's necessary in the swing. This is the objective of the next section of the book: to illustrate what to do, what not to do, and why.

PART III

• • •

SWING IDEAS TO AVOID

► 6 ◄

"The art of becoming wise is the art of
knowing what to overlook."
—*William Jones*

Say what?

*Y*ou may be wondering, is this it? Is this all there is to your system? These four SELFish parts? These very simple approaches to the swing?

You may be wondering about all the other aspects of the swing that are emphasized by many instructors. Things such as stance, tempo, and length of swing, could be what you are thinking of. You might feel that you are being robbed because I have not talked repeatedly about alignment, easy rhythm, ball position, or any of the other stuff that you are probably used to hearing. Fear not, though, you are not *"taking a bath"* with the purchase of this book.

One of the main reasons why I am so proud of what I teach is because of my "understanding" of many aspects of the swing. I do not feel that certain areas of the swing warrant the attention they are given. I believe that as long as you do what is necessary in the swing, you can approach other areas in whichever way you choose (within reason, of course).

Here is a short list of reasons why I think the way I think:

1. I have studied these parts of the swing; namely, stance, tempo, and length of swing, and noticed that just about every great non-slicing player in the world has a different approach to these parts of the swing. Therefore, it is difficult to say which player is correct.

Am I supposed to say: "Okay, Mr. Hogan, you were not very good because you swung the club so very quickly, and most people think that a slow swing is somehow better." *I don't think so.* Should I say to John Daly, "Yo J.D., give back the two major trophies you won because you wrap the club around your head, and you are supposed to be parallel at the top of your swing." *Wrong again.* Oh, wait, wait, I know. Why don't I demand that Peter Jacobsen return all of the trophies he won in 1995 because he was setting up to the ball with a bit of a closed stance, and, as you know, you need to have a perfectly parallel stance to be successful. *I think not.*

2. Because everyone is different, there is no evidence that a certain tempo, a certain stance, or a certain length of swing in any way contributes to this proper path and plane that we all must achieve. *Think about that.* How do we know that the set-up position of Lee Trevino doesn't make it any more or less difficult to establish the proper shape in the swing, as compared to the "technically superior" setup of Nick Faldo? How do we know that the long swing of Billy Andrade, or the short swing of John Cook, doesn't make it any more or less difficult to establish this proper shape, as compared to the "perfect" swing length of Ian Woosnam? How do we know that the quick tempo of Russ Cochran, or the slow tempo of Fuzzy Zoeller, doesn't make it any more or less difficult to establish this proper shape, as compared to the "superb" tempo of Tom Purtzer? All these players swing steep, then shallow, which you must do in order to hit the ball well consistently.

The only thing I have found to be common in all great non-slicing players' swings is just that: their swing shape (i.e., path and plane). They all swing outside on the backswing, then inside on the downswing, to some extent. If you, too, can simply do this in your golf swing, you are 95% on your way to becoming a good player.

3. I also realize that these areas of the swing that I don't concern myself with are *feel* oriented parts of the swing, and when you start to change things that result in making you feel uncomfortable, you're looking for trouble. We all have different feelings. We all instinctively act in certain ways in our everyday lives that make us feel at ease. The golf swing is no different.

A part of the swing such as tempo is as natural a part of us as the way we walk. It is not something that should be changed. If you naturally walk bow-legged, for instance, you can still get from point A to point B. You might look strange, but you can still get the job done. If you try to change your walk and point your toes outward, all this will do is make you feel uncomfortable. It will not make you get where you want to go any easier or better. It will probably cause you to pull a groin muscle or fall on your butt, because it is difficult to condition your mind and body to do something that doesn't come naturally.

"WAIT JUST A MINUTE THERE, JOEY," you may say. "Isn't *every* part of the swing a 'feel' aspect? Won't *any* swing change, including the ones that you suggest, make me feel uncomfortable?"

Well, maybe you're right. Maybe even the swing changes that I prescribe will make you feel awkward. I guess when you have been whipping the club over the top for so long, then are asked to change to a correct path and plane, this may feel strange at first. Or if you have been rolling the face of the club wide open for years, then all of a sudden have it square, it may feel odd as well. Let's face it, swinging with the wrong socks on might make you feel uncomfortable, let alone completely altering the structure of your swing.

Still, if you want to improve, there are some things you need to do differently. The line must be drawn somewhere on what does and does not have to be changed; on what does and does not constitute a "feel" aspect of the golf swing; and on what does and does not contribute to a slice. By observing the best players in the world, this is what I have done. I have obtained a good sense of what needs to be done in the swing, and what doesn't need to be done in the swing, from the ones who do it best.

● ● ●

Keep in mind that just because I do not focus on certain parts of a swing, does not mean that all the instruction pertaining to that aspect of the swing is wrong. Some of the best instructors in the world focus on all the pre-swing fundamentals and other characteristics of the swing that I do not. Even the famous teacher, Jim Flick, with his "Set-up for Success," and the legendary Lee Trevino, with his "TempoMaster," have developed aids and thoughts relating to areas of the swing that I do not care a lot about.

It may even help you someday to pay attention to these things, but only when you have a good path and plane structure to your golf swing. Good players can experiment with a number of unimportant aspects of the swing and know they will pretty much always hit the ball well. This is because they have excellent mechanics in their swing in regard to the essentials. If you, too, can do this, and become part of the 15% of golfers who don't swing over the top, I will set you free. You can then experiment with your stance, posture, tempo, length of swing, ball position, or whatever else. But not right now. At the stage of your slicing life, you need to focus on swing path and plane, and clubface positioning, which sounds like *The SELFish Four,* to me.

Stance

I'll admit that there has been some excellent instruction over the years in regard to stance. (No, no, I'm not sitting on the fence with this issue.) I'm sure you have heard many times about parallel lines and shoulder width. This means that your feet should be parallel to your ball-target line, and the distance between your feet should be shoulder width. This could very well be some good advice to players, but most likely to those players who are already pretty good, not to those who have an over-the-top slice. Therefore, it is not something I am too concerned with. Because, after all, I have never seen a stance that has cured an over-the-top swing path.

Over the years I have spent compiling data for this book, I have looked at some of the great, non-slicing players in the world to see how they set up to the ball. I wondered what they do with their feet and legs prior to hitting the shot. I wanted to be able to tell over-the-top slicers how they needed to stand once they were able to swing steep, then shallow. Although many of the pros stand in a normal manner, I noticed that many of them address the ball differently. There are many open, closed, wide, and narrow stances among the game's elite. Not drastically, of course, but they're still present.

I am not saying that you *should* stand like one of these players, because not one of these players is trying to stand like anyone else. What I am saying is that it is okay to have a stance that is not considered perfect. If the best in the world can do it, then so can you, as long as you have the correct shape to your swing. Nick Faldo could probably address the ball while crossing his legs and still hit good shots. This is because he has a superb shape to his swing. As a matter of fact, I have seen Nick on the range at the Buick Open hitting shots while doing one of his crazy stance drills. He was barefooted with his right foot set way behind his left, and was still hitting shots that were ten times as pure as those hit by amateurs.

Let's face it, though. We are not Nick Faldo. He is the man and we are not. You have to establish some sound mechanics before you should consider changing your stance. Once you can do that, you can then experiment with your stance on the range, or even on the course, as many pros will also do.

The reason, incidentally, that pros may adjust their stance on the course every now and then is to hit very advanced types of shots. Maybe they want to hit it low, high, low to high, high to low, with less backspin, trouble shots, a knuckle ball, or a bubble-ball. Maybe they feel that a certain stance, coupled with a particular ball position, will produce that shot, which it very well could. However, do you really think any of this stuff would help their ball striking if they were chopping at the ball from over the top? *Nor do I.*

Here are a few examples of players who address the ball in what some would consider a not-so-perfect way:

Greg Norman – When Greg won the 1993 British Open, he used quite a wide stance. It certainly wasn't shoulder width. His final round that year was considered by many as one of the finest ever. It seems that in the past couple of years since he left his teacher, Butch Harmon, he has narrowed his stance. The reason he is still great is because he has the proper moves in his swing in regard to plane. His swing is more steep and less shallow nowadays, but he still swings steep, then shallow.

Glen Day – *"Glen who?"* you might ask. Glen is a fine player on the Tour who had a good year in 1998. Up until then, videotape of Glen's swing was scarce at best. When I watched him at The Players Championship, I noticed something a little weird. His stance was so narrow! You would have thought he was just taking a practice swing or loosening up somehow before the shot, but when he actually hit the ball with that narrow a stance, I was shocked. Regardless, the guy's good.

Lee Trevino – Lee obviously has quite an open stance. He definitely doesn't concern himself with parallel lines. He also plays a draw. Don't be fooled into thinking he only plays a block with that wide-open stance. I've witnessed many draws, *even snap-hooks*, out of Lee at the Ford TPC. The reason he can play that draw is because he comes from the inside on his downswing. With that big outside-inside loop of his, Lee does practically the exact opposite of what 90% of slicers in this world do. Does that tell you something?

Peter Jacobsen – Peter has a bit of a closed stance at address. Watch him swing and notice how he drops his right foot back just before he hits. This closes his stance significantly. Peter is also a great ball striker who can shape shots any particular way.

The Bottom Line...

We have a wide, a narrow, an open, and a closed stance represented by the four players mentioned previously. Who am I to sit here and say that these golfers need to stand with feet parallel and shoulder width apart? This would be an insult to them, their methods, and their greatness. When I look at a player such as Lee Trevino, I see an excellent setup to the ball, though it seems that so many players have it in their mind that the only way to be good is to stand with feet parallel and shoulder width apart. Unfortunately, this is not what comes naturally to most people. It sure didn't for Lee when he was growing up. That's why he developed the move he did. That stance just makes it easier for him to clear his hips and come from the inside, which has resulted in his being one of the best of all time. We can all learn something from the way Lee Trevino developed his swing.

• • •

What is important to remember with all of this is that you can pretty much address the ball in any conventional way and be a good, non-slicing player. This is not just evident on the PGA Tour or any other professional tour. I'm sure you see players at your local club who are good players with weird stances. You probably wonder how somebody who stands to the ball in such an appalling way could be that good. *Guess what?* The player you see, whom I will name Ron, is just being natural.

Ron is not trying to manufacture a stance which will inhibit the rest of his body from reacting in a comfortable, natural way. Ron is not trying to impress his friends with a stance that is so fundamentally sound that he should be gracing the cover of golf annals for years to come. Instead, Ron is being Ron where Ron can be allowed to be Ron. Ron can't be Ron if his swing path and plane are as unusual as his stance, but as long as he doesn't come over the top, Ron can be himself in pretty much every other part of the swing. The point: next time you are looking for a big-money Nassau, beware of Ron with the silly stance.

Also important is that stance alone will not correct your slice. You can witness this at driving ranges all over the United States if you watch over-the-top slicers hit the ball. Some of them have what is considered "by the book" to be a very good stance. You will see them line the clubs up on the ground to make sure that they are looking professional, with a stance that is fundamentally sound, with the weight on the balls of their feet. The problem is that when they go to swing, they whip their club back to the inside, and then throw it out over the top of the ball, just like any other slicer.

What is the point of standing all pretty like that if they are going to blow it when they swing? *Hmm...*I bet they could have done that move with their old stance. They have probably been trying to improve their game, and figure they need to start with their stance to do so. I don't mean to offend anyone, but please think steep, then shallow, before you think a proper stance will do you any good.

• • •

A couple of years ago when I was slicing, I, too, thought stance might have something to do with my problem. I was just like any other slicer who opens up a book and is bombarded with stance information. I thought I finally had this slice problem solved until I heard a voice in my head one night. This voice triggered a horrifying nightmare. Let me share with you an excerpt...

Hey Joe, Hey Joe, it said in a book once to close your stance and this will get rid of your slice. Try It! Try It! Try it! "Okay," I said, "I'm going to try this in the morning. But wait, what about Fred Couples and Paul Azinger? Their stances aren't closed and they can hook it. Okay, then! An open stance is the ticket to curing a slice. But wait, what about Gil Morgan and Bob Estes? I remember seeing their feet pointing to the right of the target. Uh oh! Oh, my God! Oh, my God! Oh, my God! Okay, maybe it's a big, wide stance then. That's the key! But wait, what about Lee Janzen and Michael Bradley? Their stances sure ain't wide and they play a sweet draw. All right then, it must be a narrow stance. I've got it now! But wait, what about Moe Norman and Tiger Woods? They stand wide and they're definitely not slicers. Oh man! I'm so confu..." Beep. Beep. Beep. Beep. Beep.

• • •

HOLD EVERYTHING. I am definitely not saying *any* stance goes. Certainly, if you stand with your feet five feet apart, so close that they are touching each other, or so closed that your rear end faces the target, then you need to change. (Okay, fine. I will admit it. Stance does have a bit of relevance.) For the most part, though, if you just stand in a somewhat athletic position, you'll be fine. Besides, in order for an average player to achieve contact with the ball, he or she must have a stance that is somewhat normal and natural to begin with.

Likewise, I don't think it's too much of a stretch to think stance instruction is an insult to most people. I am sure most of us already know how it is done in the first place from all the other sports we may play. When you get in the batter's box at the family reunion softball game, do you really need someone telling you how you should stand, or do you instead just try to keep your eye on the ball and hit it? Or if you have ever played hockey, and tried to take a slapshot, you will know quickly if you have a correct stance. If you don't, you'll fall on your "hind-end."

I think the same principles can apply to golf. At least, if you consider golf a sport. You should stand adjacent to the golf ball in just as natural a way as you do at home plate. If you don't need someone telling you how to stand in the batter's box, then why do you need someone telling you how to stand next to the golf ball? Similarly, if you make a swing and fall on your butt as you did during the hockey game, you could probably assume that your stance might not be suitable. But do you really need to spend $5500 at some golf school's weekend retreat to understand this, or would trying different techniques that keep you on your feet be better?

• • •

There is one last thing that pertains to stance that I would like to mention. It has to do with how your feet point. Meaning...Do they point straight out? Do they point straight sideways? What exactly do they do?

Ben Hogan says, in *Five Lessons,* that your right foot should be square, and your left foot should be turned a quarter turn to the left. He reasoned that this square right foot would brace up your right side, and your left foot turned out would allow for your hips to rotate faster through the shot.

Then there is David Leadbetter. He says that both of your feet should point out in some manner so that your weight can rotate smoothly and you can pivot correctly, or something. I might not be exactly accurate, because in his first book he has all these measured angles and degrees and unnecessary technical stuff. Whenever I see the physics of the swing laid out in measured detail, I quickly turn the page. Though I do believe he wants both feet pointed out.

Then there is me. Your buddy from *noslice.com*. I look at what others say and scratch my head. I certainly don't laugh, because both Hogan and Leadbetter are legends of the game. I wonder, however, why so much is talked about an area of the swing that doesn't have much to do with the outcome of a golf shot; an area of the swing which is different for so many good players throughout the world; an area of the swing that, in no way whatsoever, will help over-the-top slicers get rid of their problem. All I say is stand to the ball and swing steep, then shallow.

Tempo

I believe tempo is *the* most overanalyzed aspect of the golf swing. There is no one perfect tempo, nor should there be. Every player in the world, from the Tour player to the high handicapper, has a different tempo.

Although what you will see with great players, as opposed to not-so-great players, is that they have a consistent tempo. No matter if it's super quick, or long, slow and syrupy, it's something they repeat time after time. They are not thinking "lightning strike" on one shot, and "molasses in January" on the next. That is what I am asking of you: consistency, whatever your swing tempo.

What is even more important than having a tempo that is consistent, is having one that remains natural. This naturalness is the whole essence of tempo. It is not something that can be changed, even after you do achieve the correct path and plane. Unlike stance, tempo must remain the same because you are instinctively programmed to have it that way.

Tempo is the most individual aspect of the swing. It is the glue that holds all the pieces of your swing together. If you start applying super glue to where you originally had generic school glue, your swing will be thrown out of sync. This will definitely affect your mechanics, and poor shots will result. You need to keep things in their natural harmony. If you are a naturally quick swinger of the club, you will do yourself more harm than good by swinging slow like Larry Mize. Or, if you are a naturally slow swinger of the club, you are sure to lose your entire feel by swinging fast and quick like Senior Tour player John Bland. So the key, in terms of tempo, is keeping it natural, and keeping it consistent.

• • •

A good example of why a natural tempo should not be changed is to look back at how Nick Faldo rebuilt his golf swing circa 1985.

I was recently watching some footage of a tournament in England, which took place in the early 1980s. This was the first time I had ever seen the "old" Nick Faldo swing. When I was watching him swing, it did not look all that different from how it appears today. The pace, tempo, and rhythm of his swing were basically the same.

Thus, I became confused, because it is talked so much how Nick *totally* changed his swing. It is said that when he started working with David Leadbetter, he supposedly *totally* dismantled it and put it back together. This led me to compare the two swings thoroughly and conclude the following.

The Nick of 1998 still has pretty much the same steep-then-shallow plane and tempo (rhythm) to his swing as the Nick of 1983. Because he has the essential move down already (i.e., path and plane), and he keeps consistent what he must (i.e., tempo), he is free to experiment with certain other aspects of the swing, such as pivot position, finish position, degree of dish angle, or whatever other wild ideas he has.

What Faldo has done over the years is change his body mechanics quite a bit, and that is why the shape of his swing is different today. He no longer has those crazy legs working laterally, which caused that reverse-C. Also, his torso and shoulder rotation seem a little more level these days, and he is not chicken-winging his finish nearly as much. He definitely did not, I don't think, try to speed up or slow down the most "feel" aspect of them all: tempo. This would have definitely screwed him up.

So if you're someone who simply thinks that Nick Faldo is just some *nutcase, tinkering, cybernetic, trifling, collating, mechanical, overanalyzing psycho* with regard to the swing, well then I guess you're right! Yet Nick can be this way, and will always be at least a good ball striker, if he keeps in his swing what must be there.

• • •

"So Joe, why is there so much talk in the world of golf about tempo if it means that little? Why does it seem that there are so many instructional pieces done on it if it will just screw me up?"

Believe it or not, there is some good instruction in the world of golf in regard to tempo. Stuff that instructs you how to keep a certain tempo *consistent* is good. The problem is that there is too much bad instruction in the world of golf in regard to tempo. This is stuff that instructs you on how to *achieve* a certain tempo.

This "achieving a tempo" is the basis for the entire problem that I have with tempo instruction. It's that there is widespread advice on how to speed up or slow down a tempo for a whole readership of people who don't understand that they should never, ever change their tempo in the first place. It's bad enough that most readers of instructional pieces have poor essential mechanics to begin with, let alone having them think a tempo change will do them any good.

In my opinion, all instruction on tempo or rhythm will do little good for your game, and should be ignored by you in full. Being instructed as to what tempo you should or should not be using is akin to being told what food you should like best. It doesn't make sense because it's different for everybody.

Then again, allow me to play devil's advocate for a moment. The argument could be made that all of this instruction on tempo is to help players keep things consistent, which would be good. The argument could be made that you are either a quick swinger or a slow swinger, so what could possibly be harmful with any instruction relating to those areas? I don't really buy that, though. I don't think the notion *to "turn your club upside down and make a few swings"* to speed up your tempo, or *"put a few weighted donuts around the hosel"* to slow it down, are anything more than some crazy concoctions that will do additional harm to your game.

I honestly think the only time you should consider listening to anything about tempo is if an instructor is working with you directly. If someone sees you hit four good shots swinging quickly, then on the fifth you pause at the top and shank it, allow him or her to step in and say something. Allow them to tell you not to pause, and they should give you some images for keeping the quick pace to your swing. Maybe they will tell you to feel as if you are swinging a feather duster. This could work well. However, the same advice should never be uttered to you if you have success, and feel natural, by pausing at the top of your swing (e.g., Jay Haas and Nancy Lopez). That's why tempo is so individual and must be dealt with on a person-to-person basis.

• • •

Despite the obvious differences in tempo, I fear that whatever claims I make are too little and too late. It seems as though the consensus with most people is that a slow tempo is best. Whether the average player has been brainwashed or not into thinking this way is anyone's guess, but this idea of a slow tempo must have come from somewhere. How many times have you seen a player hit a bad shot and someone say, *"Slow it down!"* They are not only referring to that player's swing speed, but also to their tempo. This notion to slow it down could potentially be some of the worst advice ever given.

Granted, it depends on what is being referred to. If you tell someone to slow down the spin out of their hips from the top of the swing, that might be okay. Being too quick with the hips can certainly lead to an over-the-top shot. On the other hand, if you tell someone to slow down the overall tempo and speed of their swing just because they hit a bad shot, you should be castigated. If anything, tell that person to swing harder, quicker, and faster than ever.

For those people who have not been brainwashed into believing that a slow tempo is best, there are those who just want their swings to look pretty. They figure if they can't score well, they might as well try to appear halfway decent. So they attempt to impress their friends with a gorgeous, sumptuous, eloquent, and, albeit unnatural, move through the ball. Why this is done is anyone's guess, but my advice would be to engage the attention of your playing partners by shooting the lowest score.

Could you imagine if Nick Price bought into this slow tempo stuff? I'm sure it was mentioned to him as a youngster to slow it down a little. *"Hey Nick, count 1-2-3-4-5 to the top, okay buddy? Then when you start down, imagine you are swinging in a swimming pool."* (That is my quote, but I'm sure something similar was uttered.) I'm sure glad Nick didn't listen to anything like this, because quick is what comes natural to him. You can't tell Nick to slow down the pace of his swing that he has been using for years. His action at Augusta in 1986, while setting the course record, was as speedy as it is today. His mechanics were a little different back then, and this is what he has improved upon over the years. He focused on building some solid mechanics around this super-quick tempo, not the other way around. He kept things natural.

On the opposite end of the tempo spectrum, there is Fred Couples. He has a very slow and smooth tempo. It basically mirrors his calm and cool demeanor. He can also produce some very fast clubhead speed with this slow, *"lava flow"* tempo. If Freddie tried to copy a fast move of, say, Ben Hogan, I don't think he would be on the Tour. Perhaps he would have still been playing baseball, which I think was his first love anyway.

Fred, just like Nick, has some excellent positions throughout his swing in regard to path and plane, and that is why he is one of the best players in the world. Take a look at a photo of Couples at waist level on the downswing, and you will understand how solid a move he has. He comes from the inside nicely and his right elbow connects to his right hip. This creates that magical gap between the forearms, which tells me, without knowing his record, that this guy is good.

Here is an insight into some other great players' tempos:

Bob Murphy — Yeah! Ya' know? The guy from the Senior Tour. If you ever get a chance to see his swing, notice how he practically stops at the top of his backswing. He has that long, slow move to the top, stops, and then fires right through. This is definitely not a move someone should copy, but it certainly works for Bob. He is a great player because he complements his natural, innate, and comfortable tempo with some excellent mechanics. I'm happy that no one convinced him to remove that pause from his swing.

Moe Norman — Moe, once again, is the legendary Canadian who is considered by many to be the best ball striker ever. I have studied his swing intensely after I became so fascinated with his story. Let me tell you that his tempo is so quick that you almost have to look at his swing in super slow motion to analyze it. He barely takes the club past waist high, then whips into the ball with laserlike precision. I sure don't think Moe would be Moe if he were thinking of "sands through an hourglass" or "swells in the ocean" while he is hitting.

Phil Mickelson — The story about Phil Mickelson is that all he worked on in his swing for his first few years on the Tour was his tempo. That's fine, for Phil. Phil already has an excellent shape to his swing. He comes from the inside beautifully, and that is why he's a tremendous player. Although Phil knows what tempo he has when he is playing his best. This is what he tries to groove on the range. I don't think Phil looks at Tommy Armour III, who has an unbelievably brisk action, and says, *"Wow, that guy* *can really hit it. I'm think I'm gonna change my tempo to super-quick."* Phil just tries to make his natural tempo as consistent as possible.

The Bottom Line...

The point in all of this is that great, non-slicing golf can be played with all sorts of swing tempos. It can be quick or slow, as long as it stays relatively consistent. What you don't want to do is swing super quick like David Edwards on one shot, and slow and smooth like Ernie Els on the next. As long as your tempo stays consistent and natural, and you also build the essential mechanics into your swing, then you will be fine.

So next time one of your playing partners tries to get you to slow down your tempo, tell him to go jump in Rae's Creek. Or, you could tell him that you are born with whatever tempo you have, and that there is nothing you can do about it. Tell him tempo is the area of the swing that is the most individual and it must remain that way. Tell him that from the moment you start playing until the moment you stop, you will pretty much have the same tempo. Tell him that when you start messing around with it, you're in trouble. Tell him one last thing...that you are going to keep the tempo you were given when you were put together in mommy's belly, and work on making it as consistent as possible.

Length of Swing

Another aspect of the swing that is so misunderstood by players is length of swing. I hear so much in the world of golf about achieving a parallel position at the top of the swing, but when I look at the top 200 players on the PGA

Tour, I get confused. I think I can count on one hand the number of players who actually achieve this parallel position at the top of their swing. It's not as though it is an isolated incident to see good players who have short or long swings. They are all over the place.

What does this all mean? Are all these great players who do not swing to parallel lucky? Should they be going to work in a suit and tie instead of khakis and a visor? Must they all bow to the golf gods and be thankful that they can play with such a lousy move? *I think not.*

These players are great because they have a length of swing which is natural to them and which they can keep consistent. It's probably the way they have been doing it forever, so by now it is just second nature. Not surprisingly, this is also what you, the slicer, need to be concerned with: trying to stick with a length of swing that is natural, and, at the same time, making it as repeatable as possible.

Who the heck cares if it's parallel? *I sure don't.* Who the heck cares if it's short of or past parallel? *I sure don't.* All I want is for you to be consistent, so you can focus on the moves of the swing that really matter. What I don't want is for you to be short like Chi-Chi Rodriguez on one shot, then wrap the club around your head like John Daly on the next. Consistency is the key.

It's important to note, however, that when I talk about having a natural and consistent length of swing, I am not presuming that every swing by a certain player will be the same length. Nor do I demand that every shot hit by a particular player must have the exact same swing length, or else they have no chance. I am instead referring to just a normal distance shot. If you are trying to rip a drive or hit a soft wedge, then your swing will be longer or shorter, accordingly. This is fine. This is just a natural, physical reaction to your mental image of the shot. This is just your body's way of balancing what needs to be done in order to hit the ball longer or shorter than what is considered normal. This also relates to the fact that trying to rip a drive or hit a half wedge is more difficult, because of how you need to alter your natural length of swing to do so.

• • •

Here is a short list of great players whose top-of-backswing position is not parallel with the ground:

Long	Short
John Daly	Tom Lehman
Tom Watson	John Cook
Justin Leonard	Tiger Woods
Phil Mickelson	Moe Norman
Steve Stricker	Tommy Armour III
Gil Morgan	John Jacobs
Shigeki Maruyama	Jim Furyk
David Duval	Lee Trevino
Brent Geiberger	Ted Tryba
Colin Montgomerie	Chi-Chi Rodriguez
David Toms	Mark O'Meara
Robert Damron	Allen Doyle

These players may have different swing lengths, but they all have something in common in their swings. *You guessed it!* They all swing steep, then shallow.

• • •

What boggles my mind is when I see people instructing others to get the club in that mythical "parallel slot" at the top of the swing. I'm sure you see it all the time as well. The teacher or friend will take the person's club and help them swing it back into this position, so as to illustrate how this move is done. Or they will grab the player's shoulders and say something such as, *"All right now, Billy Bob, turn your shoulders away from the ball to the perpendicular position. You should feel like you put your left shoulder underneath your chin. Once you do that, your club will be in a lovely, parallel position at the top."* This sure sounds great, but what they forget to tell Billy Bob is that once he gets into this position and feels extremely uncomfortable, unnatural, stiff, inelastic, rigid, and out of balance, he must now swing down.

What questionable advice this truly is, not to mention a big waste of time. There is no length of swing that you, or Billy Bob, should ever be instructed to achieve. Unless you have a length of swing that is so appalling that it *must* be dealt with—which, if you do, will probably result in a whiff anyway—I don't think it would be wise for you to entertain the thought of changing it. If any aspect of "length of swing" is considered, it should be about making your normal and natural swing length as consistent as possible, and it doesn't take two brains to figure out that being taught something that is natural to you will defeat the whole purpose.

I guess swing-length instruction should be approached in the same manner as tempo instruction. If someone sees you hit some good shots while swinging the club back to waist high, but you chunk the next one because you went way past parallel, allow them to say something. I hope they will advise you on what length of swing appears natural to you and produces good results. I hope they will acknowledge that going past parallel is not what's in your best interest, and I hope they will give you some ideas to stop it. Perhaps they will tell you to point the butt end of the club more at the ground instead of the sky at the top of your swing. This would be something to keep in mind. I just hope they don't tell John Daly this same stuff.

• • •

Swing length is also brought up quite a bit when talking about distance. This is when average players freak out. They think that they have to swing the club long in order to hit it far. In order to impress their buddies with a monster drive, they will wrap the club so far around their cranium that they can see it out of the corner of their left eye.

I was reading a "Letter to the Editor" in a golf magazine a couple of years ago when this subject came up. Whoever wrote this piece was comparing the golf swing to a slingshot. The point was the following: *"The farther you pull the slingshot back, the farther the rock will travel. Consequently, the farther you swing the club back, the farther the ball will travel."*

On the surface, this person makes sense, but only on the surface. This guy must never have seen John Jacobs or Tommy Armour III play. Both of these men barely get the club past waist level and are a couple of the longest hitters in the world. Maybe whoever wrote this has never seen Justin Leonard and Larry Mize play. Both of them swing the club long and a little past parallel and are near the bottom of the list for driving distance.

There are a lot of factors that can go into how far you hit the ball, but if you look at the best players in the world, you will see that length of swing is one of the most insignificant. Tiger gets his power from his unbelievably fast rotation through the shot. He sets the club at the top with a ridiculous amount of coil, then absolutely rips through the ball with his hips. Seve gets his distance from his hinging and unhinging of his wrists. This allows for him to wait until the last second to release, which results in a surge of clubhead speed through impact. Tom Lehman hits it long because he de-lofts each club at impact, allowing for increased distance from an otherwise normally lofted club. None of these long hitters relies on swinging *longer* in order to hit the ball far.

• • •

Another disturbing thing is when I see certain Tour players changing the length of swing that got them to where they are in the first place. ON THE TOUR! I don't know if they are convinced by instructors to do this, or if it is their decision. Whatever the case, it usually doesn't work.

I think a good example of a player who has fallen victim to this line of thinking is Phil Mickelson. I know I said earlier that Phil only works on his tempo. That was when Phil was younger and was really, really, good. Now he is just really good, because he has started to focus on some areas of his swing that will do nothing but confuse him, such as length of swing.

Phil used to have a swing that went quite a bit past parallel. When he used that swing, he dominated. He won a host of amateur events (he even won a PGA Tour event as an amateur) and had some great success during his first few years on the Tour. It seems that in the last couple of years, he has tried to shorten his swing. He feels that this shorter swing will help him create a more shallow, level approach into the ball and produce less backspin. He reasons this will help him in the major championships.

His theory on this may be absolutely correct. I would have to give him an "A" for his analysis of the objective, but I don't agree with the change. What's the point of trying to obtain this when it takes such an alteration of a "feel" aspect of the swing? He should stick with what brought him to where he is in the first place and improve naturally.

He was better at age sixteen than he was at fourteen with his natural move. He was better at nineteen than he was at sixteen by improving on his natural move and abilities. He was better when he first came out on the Tour than he was at nineteen by continuing to work on and improve the natural aspects of his swing. What makes him think he can't keep on improving with the swing length he has, to the point where he can become a major championship winner? Why does he need to shorten it up? Hey Phil, John Daly and Corey Pavin have never thought about shortening their swings, and they have three majors between them.

Phil must understand that this is not a part of the game that suits his natural ability. His strengths are his distance off the tee and his putting. When he is long and loose with the driver, he can bomb it. When he is long and loose with the putter, he can make anything he looks at. He won't be effective in these areas if he thinks mechanics and acts robotic, and, as a result, shortens his swing.

"Where went the Phil I have come to know and love?" I ask myself these days. I notice how out of sync he becomes when he tries to make that short swing, and how poorly he has putted since he has worked on that newer move. This

shorter swing has definitely filtered down to some problems with the flat stick.

Do you remember Phil Mickelson's putting when he first came out of college? It was unbelievable. He made everything. He not only made everything, but he did so in a pure-as-hell way. And yet as gifted a putter as Phil is, have you ever seen someone miss more short putts over the past couple of years than *"Mick"*? It's disturbing to watch because I want so badly for him to play well, but when he lines up that 3-5 footer, I can almost tell that he is going to miss it before he strokes it.

Go back to your old-self, Phil, and wrap the club around your head, so you can realize the potential that you have.

• • •

Someday, maybe shortening or lengthening your swing might be a good thing. I haven't seen any evidence of that helping anyone, but maybe you will be the Chosen One for that to happen to. Maybe you will be the one that all the parallel cronies had in mind when they thought of such a position. Worry about such tinkering only when you are doing what is necessary in the swing. Why bother checking the price of the newest Porsche when you are still working at the grocery store? You can cross that bridge when you come to it.

Conclusion

Stance, tempo, and length of swing are misunderstood aspects of the golf swing. What's important for you to note is that changing any of them will not eliminate your slice. It will, most of the time, just make things worse, because it will throw off your entire natural sequence of motion.

Just about every good player in the world approaches these areas differently. This tells me, and it should probably tell you, that the stance, tempo, and length of swing you currently have are fine. As long as they are not too abnormal, you should leave them alone. They are, most likely, adequate enough to allow for you to get rid of your slice, and hit the ball well, as long as you can build the necessary components into your swing.

Certainly, there is the talent factor that comes into play. Just because you develop the most beautiful inside path into the ball does not automatically mean that you will be a fine player. You must understand, though, that in order to become good, you must first have this move. You do not need a perfectly parallel and shoulder-width stance. You do not need a slow and easy tempo. You do not need a parallel clubshaft at the top of your swing. But as you can see by watching any good ball striker, you do need the correct path and plane.

► 7 ◄

"The whole point of getting things done is
knowing what to leave undone."
—*Lady Reading*

*T*he three parts of the swing that were just talked
about—stance, tempo, and length of swing—are the most
misunderstood of all. These are the areas in the swing that
are so overly taught to the average golfer that it's actually
rather disgusting. However, there are other parts of the
swing in addition to these that are confusing, and give
instructors and players fits trying to figure out.

I don't want to stray too much from the fact that this is
a book for slicers, so I must mention the following
disclaimer statement before I can proceed: *"Hey, Mr. Over
the Top Slicer, nothing else matters in your swing until you*

can get a steep, then shallow swing path and plane structure." Nevertheless, it's important to mention a few more things that we all need to understand about the swing.

Grip

Have you ever seen a player getting a lesson who is not told to alter their grip somehow? *Nor have I.* Have you ever seen that player feel at all comfortable, and happy, with the change? *Nor have I.* Why does this part of the swing have to be talked about so repeatedly if changing it will simply annoy us and throw our entire, natural motion out of whack? *Who knows?*

For the most part, I am a not a stickler on the grip. I am somewhat for the open-clubface-at-impact slicer because of the two reasons I stated in the last section. A weak grip usually equals an open clubface, and a weak grip is atypical with the game's best. Even so, one of the main reasons why I don't like to change the player's grip too much is because it is such a "feel" aspect of the swing, not only in the full swing, but also in the short game.

You can't just nonchalantly suggest to people to change things that make them feel extremely uncomfortable. The way you set your hands on the club is the way that makes you feel good, relaxed, and in a position to make an aggressive swing. PGA Tour player Ed Fiori feels good with that unbelievably strong grip of his (the guy's nickname is "gripper"), Curtis Strange also feels good with the weak grip that he employs, and Sammy, the local 21-handicapper, feels good with that thing that he calls a grip. So whatever the case, whoever the human, personal preference is a key with regard to the grip.

The grip is not that unlike tempo. It's certainly not as ingrained in the traits of your overall being as much as tempo is, but the entire natural makeup of your swing can be destroyed if you make drastic changes to it. You can't go to a weak grip to play a fade, or to a super-strong grip to play a hook. Sorry, but things don't work that way. You have to make changes in the truly *mechanical* aspects of the swing, not the *feel* aspects.

That is where I would rather see a change made: in your mechanics. I would much prefer seeing some increased leg action needed through impact to hit the ball straight, than I would for you to have to weaken your grip to hit it straight, or I would prefer to see you come more from the inside to hit a draw, than to see you strengthen your grip, if that change would completely screw you up. Anything to keep intact the sensory aspects of the swing makes me happy.

You will also notice this with the pros when they make changes in their golf swing. They rarely change such a "feel" part of the swing as the grip. They would much favor a change in something such as their body movement, alignment, knee flex, ball position, or, in Nick Faldo's case, *width of downswing lever angle,* instead of changing the way their hands are placed on the club. They understand that any change in the grip will affect every single part of their game, almost always in the negative.

I know that when I was playing junior golf, I was told all the time that my grip was much too strong. Maybe, according to conventional standards, it was. Every now and then, when I would try to weaken it a little, my whole swing would be thrown out of kilter. My somewhat smooth tempo became all jerky, and my whole feel for the shot completely escaped me. Because of this, I looked at what I was doing, and realized that I could play most of the shots already because I had a decent inside move into the ball. Therefore, I was going to keep the things in my swing that felt comfortable—such as grip and tempo—and change my angle of attack when I needed to hit different types of shots. I would do something such as "clear my hips hard and swing left of the target" to play a fade, or I would "swing across my body more" to play a hook. There was no changing of the intricate aspects of the swing. Instead, I focused on the larger muscles of the chest, torso, hips, and legs when I had to maneuver the ball.

This weak grip also affected my short game a great deal. I was chunking and blading shots all over the place when I tried to change my grip on a chip shot or pitch shot. If I did manage to make clean contact, the ball would absolutely explode off my clubface, and go thirty feet past the hole, because I had lost all feel for the shot.

• • •

Another reason why I stay away from changing the grip is because just about every player in this world has a different grip. We all have different hand and grip sizes to go with our different feelings of how to place our hands on the club. All of these differences will almost certainly result in each of us having a different grip.

This is not only obvious for the weekend hackers, but also for the professionals. Some of the best ball strikers in the world have completely different grips. There is Jose-Maria Olazabal, who has a weak grip, and Ben Crenshaw, who has a strong grip. They are both Masters champions, so obviously they both must be good. How can you look at their grips and necessarily say that one is good and one is bad? Would you not be disregarding Ben by saying a player must have a weak grip like Jose's in order to be good?

There are also some extreme grips out on the Tour that most people would be shocked at. Look at David Duval, for instance. He is one of the best players in the world and has as strong a grip as you could possibly have. His hands are turned so far underneath the club that he has to clear his hips in a pronounced way to avoid a hook. His clubface is so closed at the top of his swing that you could practically set a cup of coffee on it. Still, even with a grip that every stodgy golfing mind would call lousy, Mr. Duval could end up being one of the best players of all time.

• • •

Although it's pretty obvious that many pros are different, what you will see in common with most good players in the world today is some form of a *strong* grip. They essentially just differ in *how strong* their grip is, not whether it's strong or weak. This is why I am not afraid to tell golfers that it would be in their best interest if they did it as well. If it's good enough for about 90% of pros, chances are that it will be good enough for you, too.

Basically what this means is that they have their hands, especially the left one, turned to the right in some degree. This strong left hand creates a lot of leverage in the swing and a very powerful release through the ball, which, in turn, creates distance. Not to mention, if you look at all the long hitters on the PGA Tour, it is almost a guarantee that you will see a strong grip. There are John Daly, Scott McCarron, Tim Herron, John Adams, and, of course, Tiger Woods. They all have a relatively strong grip.

Actually, in terms of how a grip can increase distance, maybe it would be better to look at the short hitters. Most of them have weak grips, with the "V's" pointing somewhere around their chin. Curtis Strange and Olazabal have weak grips and they are fairly short off the tee. Then there is Corey Pavin, who has a very weak grip, and Corey is very short off the tee. It's really hard for these players to get that *late release snap* at impact with such a weak grip.

So grip it strong, hit it long, and you can't go wrong. Having said that, let's move on....

Grip Pressure

"Like you are holding onto a bird, Suzie. Strong enough to keep it from flying away, but not so strong that you may hurt it."

"Pretend it's a helium balloon, Richie. Don't let it go into the air, but don't pop it, either."

Do these examples sound familiar to you? How many times do we have to hear these tired illustrations? Images like these absolutely bore the heck out of me. They make me think of golf not as a cool sport, but as a tedious diversional activity.

It really does take all my energy to keep on reading something when I come across some "grip pressure smak." It definitely takes all the fun out of the game when you cannot even *touch* a club without someone barking instructions at you. I mean really, can we not have at least one area of the swing that doesn't need perusing? Can we not have at least one area of the swing for which there is no training gadget?

But I am not going to worry about it. *No way!* Nor am I going to get upset and say that all the thoughts pertaining to grip pressure are useless, because what's the point after all. I am tired of doing this stuff with such meaningless aspects of the swing. I would rather have acupuncture done on my eyeballs than to keep on rehashing this stuff. People should really know better by now.

People should know that when Tiger Woods is going for the 18th green at Pebble Beach on his second shot, that he's probably not saying to himself, *"Gee, if I can just get my grip pressure correct, I think I can pull it off."* When Seve Ballesteros is going to hit some amazing recovery shot from the trees, he's more than likely not uttering, *"Man o' man, if I can just hold onto that bird without smushing it, I may have a chance."* At the 1986 Masters, when Jack Nicklaus was sizing up his heroic shot on the 16th hole, it's a good bet that he wasn't thinking to himself, *"Okay now, Jack, forget about picking out a target and making a good aggressive swing, but instead feel like you're shaking a woman's hand."*

● ● ●

I have an idea. I think I know how you and I can keep things normal and fun in golf. I think if we can divert all this grip-pressure stuff away from golf and into other areas of life, this will keep our game enjoyable.

*I say...*we tell every student throughout the country that they should grip the pen soft, like they are holding Jell-O, in order to write effectively.

*I say...*we tell everyone at the supermarket to grip the cart as though they are riding a bike, so it makes it easier to turn up and down the aisles.

*I say...*we go to a hockey rink and tell players to imagine they are wringing a wet rag as they are taking a slapshot.

*I say...*we go to a gym and instruct people who are climbing rope that they should grip the rope hard enough to where they see their biceps flex.

If these things sound stupid, *it's because they are!!*

The point is this: I DON'T need someone to tell me how hard to grip a pen. I DON'T need someone to tell me how hard to grip a shopping cart. I DON'T need someone to tell me how hard to grip a hockey stick. And I sure as heck DON'T need someone to tell me how hard to grip a rope that I am trying to climb. So why do I constantly need someone telling me how hard to grip a golf club? I am guessing that this will come just as naturally as anything else.

If the club flies out of my hands, this might tell me that I am not gripping it hard enough. If veins start popping out of my head, this could be an indication that I am gripping it too hard. If neither of these things happens, I can thereupon cogitate that the capacity with which I embrace the club is suitable for good play. And to think this could be realized without dropping big money at a golf school...truly amazing!

Oh, yeah. I almost forgot. There is one final thought that I would like to add concerning this grip-pressure issue. I can honestly say that out of the thousands of golf balls I have hit in my life, and of the zillions of swing thoughts I have used while hitting those balls, I have never once thought of grip pressure. Not when I started, not when I was reworking my swing, not when I used to be somewhat good, never. Because I have never thought of grip pressure in my entire life, and have hit some decent shots along the way, I have come up with my own swing thought for it...*PUT YOUR HANDS ON THE CLUB AND SWING!*

Pre-shot Routine

"Huh?" I know. I don't want to talk about it, either. I do, however, feel obligated to share my thoughts. Some people feel that they need to do a certain kind of routine to hit the ball better. Some people feel that they can find in a book what makes *them* get ready, set, and in a good frame of mind to hit the shot. *Whoa!*

Oh, boy, I don't even know where to start with this issue. Has anyone ever seen two pre-shot routines that are the same? *Nor have I.* (I should probably stop right now.) The only thing that matters in the pre-shot routine is that you aim the clubface and the ball at the target. Whatever else you do is totally up to you.

It doesn't matter if you stand on your head for a couple of seconds, comb your hair and put deodorant on, or smack your ankle with your club a few times. As long as you can do it over and over again, it's as good a routine as anyone else's. Incidentally, the more unorthodox it looks, the more habitual it probably is.

Have you ever seen Senior Tour player Bruce Summerhays address the ball? How anyone could develop something like that is hard to believe. He bounces the club all over the place for a few seconds before he hits. It's amazing that he doesn't accidentally hit the ball with all of those weird gyrations. How about Bob Tway? He stands behind the ball, grips the club with his left hand, then starts grasping it all over the place with his right hand. You would have thought that his leather-wrap grip was unraveling and this was an attempt to keep it adhered. Then there is Wayne Levi. Wayne stands like an absolute rock for about ten seconds before he takes the club back. There is literally no movement whatsoever. He might be breathing, but that's about it. There are certainly no essential waggles that supposedly all good players must have.

What's important to note with all these great players' routines is that it's something they can do over and over again. Whether it's during a pro-am with a bunch of bean counters, or on the 72nd hole of a major championship, it's always the same thing. It's always something they can fall back on to put themselves in their comfort zone.

Also note how each routine seems so strange that there is almost no way it could have been copied from someone else. I would have to believe that they were simply developed instinctively and reinforced over a number of years of playing. As a result, it is not something they have to think about on a shot-to-shot basis. It seems to occur automatically, and this makes it all the more easy for them to be in a good mindset to hit the shot.

● ● ●

In addition to golf, what you will find in most sports is that having a pre-shot routine that is natural to that particular athlete, even if it may look weird, is the best way. Whether it's a basketball player at the free-throw line, a football player lining up a field goal, or a tennis player getting ready to serve, the ones who keep their act intuitive and consistent will have the best chance of succeeding.

I was watching a Boston Red Sox baseball game recently when Nomar Garciaparra came up to hit. I was totally amazed by what I saw. He was flipping his feet all over the place while in the batter's box. He would raise his heels up and tap his toes into the ground repeatedly before the pitcher threw the ball. It was something I had never seen. It was actually kind of funny looking.

Guess what? This is Nomar's pre-swing routine. This is what makes him feel ready, set, and in a good frame of mind to hit the ball. This is not something he read in a book or tried to copy from another player. This is just what he developed over time. As the pitch was on its way and it was time to swing, the feet settled down and he was in great shape to hit the ball, just as any other all-star hitter.

Keep this in mind when you develop your pre-shot routine in golf. It can be unusual and look funny, as long as it's repeatable. You don't need to force yourself to do something so you will look professional and be accepted by your playing partners. You don't even need to look at what your favorite pro is doing and try to copy that. *You don't need to squint your eyes five million times the way Lee Janzen does. You don't need to confirm your yardage 200 times as Fred Couples does. You don't need to do a waltz the way Nick Faldo does. You don't even have to crook your neck a thousand times the way Tom Lehman does.* You want to keep as many things as natural and comfortable as they can be. This will make it so much easier to do it over and over again, which is the most important thing anyway.

● ● ●

I can give you a good example of why it should not be in your best interest to copy someone else's pre-shot routine. It has to do with a buddy of mine I played with on the Colorado State golf team years back named Jim Williamson. Jim was a really cool guy and a solid player, but it absolutely pained us teammates watching him set up to the ball. He copied Jack Nicklaus's routine "to the T." I mean, it was the exact same thing. Every waggle was timed precisely. He picked out the spot-target in front of the ball with the same glare as did Jack. Sure enough, he even did that trademark Nicklaus head swivel to start the swing. It was amazingly eerie that someone could duplicate a pre-shot routine that well.

At times I think this routine hurt Jim because it was *so* manufactured. He would concentrate so hard on perfecting every minute detail of the routine, that I think he didn't always concentrate on hitting the shot. You could tell every now and then that he wasn't in a comfortable position to proceed with the swing. This may also explain why he would hit a few shots well, then the next one off the map.

On top of what I saw with Jim, I don't see many good players these days copying their boyhood idols. I'm sure many of the young guys on the Tour idolized Palmer and Hogan and Player, but you don't see them copying their pre-shot routines. Every pro has his or her way of getting ready to hit the shot. Every pro has his or her way of relaxing and steadying the nerves. Every pro has his or her way of achieving peak concentration. That's the way it should be for you, too. It's all about what makes you most comfortable and ready to hit a golf shot.

Posture

Posture is an area of the swing that is also different for a lot of good players. Make no mistake; it is important to have decent posture. A major reason why postures look so different is because of all the different heights, arm lengths, and leg lengths among golfers, but if you study their swings, you will notice they are pretty much the same in regard to their posture. Therefore, there are a couple of things that will be helpful for you to know.

Don't worry! I'm not going to fill your head with stuff pertaining to knee flex, arms hanging freely, or sticking your butt out. You won't even hear me mention something about placing a sword under your throat in order to keep your chin up. All of these things will do more harm than good if you focus on them. There is one thing, albeit, that I would like to mention, and that is your spine angle, because I think it has some importance.

Any moron, myself included, can figure out that golf is played on a tilted plane with the ball on the ground. Because it is played on a tilted plane, with the ball on the ground, your body must somehow tilt so you can reach the ball. This is different in baseball. Baseball is played on a more level plane because the ball is struck somewhere around waist high. This is why baseball players stand in a more vertical position with their back straight. Then there are tennis players. When they hit a serve, the ball is hit while it is above their head. It is pretty clear that these players must tilt backward to get to that object which is above their head.

Believe it or not, there is a point behind this obvious pabulum. When I was in the midst of destroying my game in early 1996, I had the audacity to believe that my back (spine angle) should be in a vertical position at address. I believed the feeling should be similar to riding a horse or standing in a batter's box. I studied dozens of photographs of baseball players, trying to see the similarities between their posture and a golfer's. I believed that the way to get down to the ball was to pinch my knees in until I was there.

"What the hell was I thinking?" I ask myself nowadays. To say the laws of physics would be defied with a vertical spine would be an understatement. To say that common sense would take a massive hit would be more accurate than that. To say that you would lose your balance would be even more accurate. To say that you would look like a total idiot may be the most accurate of them all. So you need to tilt, or your body may wilt.

• • •

The point I'm trying to make is that having at least some degree of an angled spine is important. What measure of tilt you have in your swing is up to you, because there is no one formula. You certainly don't have to whip out the protractor to make sure that your spine angle complies. If you are extremely bent over, this is not necessarily bad, no matter what anyone says. There are some good players out on the Tour who have quite a bit of tilt, so I'm guessing that this means you can, too.

I was watching the Buick Classic last year and saw Kevin Sutherland's set-up position for the first time. I couldn't believe how bent over from the waist this guy was. Granted, most pros are not *that* extreme. *He looked like Pac-Man!* Nonetheless, he held that position nicely throughout his swing and was hitting some great shots. By keeping that angle the same, he can be effective with such an extreme posture.

That's the key. Keep whatever angle you set at address as consistent as possible. Losing your spine angle can lead to some seriously bad moves in the swing. Chunks, tops, whiffs, skulls, shanks, pop-ups, chili-dips, etc., all become possibilities. You can also have the tendency to commit the most deadly sin of all if you come up and out of your spine angle, and that's swing the club over the top.

Maintaining this spine angle, by the way, is a key ingredient for over-the-top slicers to incorporate into their swing, especially the players who swing over the top from throwing their right shoulder out. A constant spine angle will get their right shoulder working *under* the plane, as opposed to throwing it out *over* the plane. If their spine is set too vertical, they will not have enough room to do this. Their right side will have no choice but to be thrown outward if they want to swing down and make contact with the ball.

If you get the chance, watch Tom Kite hit balls. His spine is set on a great angle, and he keeps that angle as steady throughout the swing as anyone I have ever seen. Also notice when he finishes his swing, how he really holds that angle for a long time. This is to reinforce to himself and his brain to never come up and out of a shot.

Tom is not riding a horse. Tom is not doing a military press. Tom is not holding a 50-pound sack of potatoes. Tom is playing a sport where the ball happens to be resting on the ground, and one that requires a tilted spine. Tom also happens to be a very tidy, non-slicing player.

Weight Distribution

"The balls of your feet. The balls of your feet. Stand with your weight on the balls of your feet."

NOOOOOOO KIDDDDDDING! Gee, I thought I was supposed to put all my weight toward my toes so I would eventually fall on my face. Better yet, I was considering leaning so far back on my heels so I would leave huge indentations in the ground.

Am I hallucinating, or have people actually tried to tell others that they need to stand with the weight on the balls of their feet? To tell human beings who already know how to stand, walk, and run, that they need to have the weight on the balls of their feet when they are preparing to do an athletic activity, is something I will never understand.

I don't want to go off on a rant here and say that you would never tell infielders to keep the weight on the balls of their feet; that you would never tell quarterbacks to keep the weight on the balls of their feet; that you would never tell tennis players to keep the weight on the balls of their feet, or that you would never tell a 65-pound, 11-year-old Olympic gymnast performing on the balance beam to keep the weight on the balls of her feet. I'm guessing that anyone with an IQ of at least 10 will know this will come natural to these athletes.

But this stuff does need to be addressed. Someone does need to bring it to the forefront. Someone does need to relate certain areas of golf to other sports; that is, if golf wants to continue to be a sport. It can't be if there is constant analysis of something so manifest to athletic competition as weight distribution. Anyone who plays golf, as well as any other sport, knows where the weight should be distributed, and anyone with a cerebellum within their skull is able to achieve it.

All I know is that if I were ever to get a tennis lesson about how to volley at the net, I would bet the house that I would not be told how to distribute the weight through my feet. The instructor might tell me how to hold the racket, how to position the racket, and how to swing the racket in order to improve my shot, but he would take for granted that I understand that in order to be ready to receive the shot, I would need to have the weight on the balls of my feet.

This is where the weight-distribution problem lies in regard to golf. Why does it have to be lectured in golf if it is taken for granted in every other sport? Why can't golf be held in the same light as all the other sports I see on ESPN? Why does every part of the game have to be measured in scientific detail? Why can't certain athletic fundamentals be left alone in golf so we can all concentrate on what's actually important?

I guess what I am getting at is this...*Why do I need some stupid, dogaan, flippin', livin' electronic sensor training gadget placed in my shoe to tell me that the weight is on the balls of my feet? DAMN IT!*

WHOA-WHOA-WHOA-WHOA!!!!!!!!!
Take it easy, Joe!

I apologize for the outburst. That was very unprofessional of me and totally uncalled for. If it sounds as though I am starting to get upset, it's because I am. As a matter of fact, I think I am about ready to snap. But it's for a good reason. It's because any discussion that insults basic common sense tends to freak me out, and anything emphasized other than what is absolutely vital to the golf swing tends to freak me out even more, especially when it is geared toward over-the-top slicers. These players have rarely had a chance to enjoy the game because they continue to loop it inside, then hack it outside. They shouldn't have to be insulted, and at the same time, start to worry about an aspect of the golf swing which should come as natural to them as standing in the shower.

I will not let it happen to them. I will not let them go down the same road I went down. I will not let them fight the same wars I fought. I will not let them feel the shame I felt. I will not let them embarrass themselves the way I did. I will not let them be confused the way I was. In other words, I will not let anything other than what's absolutely critical to their success enter their mind, and that includes weight distribution. Put your feet on the ground and find yourself a good swing plane.

Balance

First of all, what is balance? Is balance being able to stand in place after hitting a shot? Is balance being able to stand in place with the weight on the balls of your feet after hitting a shot? Is balance being able to stand in place with the weight on the balls of your feet and the angle of your clubshaft matching the angle of your spine that you had set at address, after hitting a shot?

I suppose all of these could qualify for defining what balance is. They certainly could work, I guess, as an answer to the great balance question in the golf swing. Regardless of the definition, though, what is important to note with balance is nothing. Good balance is something that will either happen or not happen, depending on what you do in your swing. Just as the weight shift should happen automatically, so should balance.

If you make an exaggerated reverse pivot, you are not going to maintain good balance. If you whip the club way to the inside going back, and throw it way to the outside coming down, it's a good bet that you will lose your balance. If you shift laterally a great deal on the backswing, and laterally a great deal on the downswing, you will probably be "de-balanced" somewhere along the way. Still, good balance is not that hard to achieve. All you have to do is make a good swing.

As you stand to the ball, you are probably in good balance, unless you like leaning all over the place. If you start your swing by taking the club on the correct path and plane, you will not only achieve a proper weight shift, but your backswing will be in balance. From there, if you drop everything into the slot and swing down from the inside, your lower body will shift and your upper body will stay back, and you will be balanced at impact. Because you automatically shifted your weight to your right leg on the backswing, this good impact position should automatically create a shift to your left leg after you hit the ball. *Voila! You're in balance.*

This is what should happen, and, for the most part, does with good players. Their weight starts off equally on both feet, then automatically shifts to the inside of their right leg going back. From there they arrive at impact in good balance, and then finish with about 85% of their weight on their left leg, with their right foot spikes showing. Also, their backs straighten out after impact, as the reverse-C is becoming a thing of the past. They appear to "pose for a picture," as some like to say.

•••

As always, there are a few good players who don't conform to this. There are some players, who, despite having excellent mechanics, don't finish in good balance. There are some players out there who like to disprove my whole theory on how certain things in the swing work.

Take Dave Stockton, for example. For as great a player as Dave is, I sometimes forget how much of an eyesore bad balance is until I see him swing. For someone who has such good shape to his swing, it is alarming to me that he practically falls on his rear end after each shot. What is even more worrisome is how he almost falls on his rear end from a relatively easy swing. Could you imagine if he took a "Tiger-esque" lash at the ball? He would probably get tossed three fairways over, or maybe he would screw himself right into the ground. Yet Dave's really a stand-up guy. *Whoops!* Maybe that was a poor choice of words. What I meant to say is that Dave is a real class act with a record that speaks for itself. He certainly doesn't need my two cents' worth of advice on maintaining balance.

Wouldn't it be great, though, if all golfers had the balance of Steve Elkington? Wouldn't it be nice if we could all look like "the Elk"? Is it not truly awesome to watch him hit balls? Does it not look like he could keep his balance even during a tornado? How he doesn't win more tournaments is beyond me. It's incredible that someone could have that good rhythm and flow to their swing.

And yet even if we can't all have what Steve has, it's at least a good idea to keep this image of his balance in mind. It will probably give you a good feel for his superb mechanics as well. Notice how he doesn't achieve this good balance by rolling the clubface open on the backswing. Notice how he doesn't achieve it by looping the club inside on the way back, then throwing it outside on the way down. Notice how he doesn't achieve it by collapsing his left arm in a 90-degree angle at the top of the swing. Notice how he doesn't achieve it by sliding his weight eight inches on the backswing, then fourteen inches on the downswing. *But please, please, please, do notice how he swings steep, then shallow.*

Conclusion

From senseless, to SELFish, to sarcastic, I think I have pretty much covered everything. It has been an interesting journey, but it must end sometime. I hope you have enjoyed it and can learn from it.

Believe it or not, behind some of the theatrics, there is a message that I want to convey. I honestly do feel that all slicers can improve if they are willing to change. It's more of a mental change than anything. The golf swing does not have to be as complex as brain surgery, unless someone wants it to be. It should be no different than driving a car. It's just a matter of doing a few things correctly, and keeping your eye on the road.

Keeping your eye on the road is crucial for a slicer. In my opinion, once you are a slicer, you are always a slicer. You have to keep reminding yourself of this or you could regress. You have to keep reminding yourself of what the essential moves are in the swing, and you have to keep working on them with the utmost determination.

I keep my eye on the road all the time. Although these days I hit more hooks than slices, I still consider myself a slicer. One thing's for certain and it's that I don't want to go back. I know I won't go back as long as I focus on the important parts of the golf swing, and leave all the rest alone. I think you will be better off if you do the same.

• • •

As I leave you, allow me to share this Irish blessing that I use as my slicers' creed. As we all know, slicers have been treated most unfairly over the years. On top of playing awful golf, we have been flooded with enigmas about various aspects of the game, and seemingly forced to abide by them. Why this is, I have no idea. It was not our choice to be this way, nor should it be someone else's choice that we remain this way.

This creed, or "modo," relates to anyone who tries to interrupt our path with their widespread innuendoes:

> May those that love us, love us.
> And those that don't love us,
> May God turn their hearts.
> And if He doesn't turn their hearts,
> May He turn their ankles
> So we will know them by their limping.

Take care.
Play well.

In addition to authoring this book, Joseph K. Sullivan has produced a video: *Stop Your Slice with The SELFish Four.* He also publishes a free, weekly, e-lesson newsletter at his website: www.noslice.com.